D0544078

URBAN SPIRITUALITY

Embodying God's Mission in the Neighborhood

Karina Kreminski

Urban Loft Publishers | Skyforest, CA

Urban Spirituality
Embodying God's Mission in the Neighborhood

Senior Editors: Stephen Burris & Kendi Howells Douglas
Copy Editor: Marla Black
Graphics: Amber Craft

ISBN-13: 978-0-9989177-2-6

Made in the U.S.

Praise for *Urban Spirituality*

Karina Kreminski is no armchair mission scholar. She is a reflective practitioner who maps out a vision for inventive urban ministry in our post-Christendom world. This ministry is informed by the biblical narratives, grounded in spiritual practices, marked by gentle community engaging strategies, and a risk-taking openness to the guiding Spirit. This winsome book may well become a key resource for new ways in engaging in urban ministry in our secular age.
>   -Charles Ringma, Emeritus Professor, Mission Studies, Regent
>   College, Vancouver

Urban Spirituality is a contemporary expression of Jeremiah 29:7 "Seek the welfare of the city for in its welfare you will find your welfare." It reminds us how our own spiritual lives and the spiritual life of the city are interwoven, inviting us into a way of life that watches for God's work in ourselves and our city. It dares us to trust that if we let ourselves be transformed by the way God is at work in our city, we may become the message we so desperately long to share with our neighbors
>   -Mandy Smith, pastor and author of *The Vulnerable Pastor*

Karina Kreminski views urban spirituality with fresh new eyes. As a suburban pastor recently relocated to the city, she is learning the rhythms of her community and seeking to discover what God is doing there. This gives her a less jaded, more optimistic view of urban ministry that's bound to re-inspire old timers and enliven those, like her, who are new to the city.
>   -Michael Frost, author of *Surprise the World* and *To Alter Your World*

The Church globally is in consternation. The cool church growth techniques that worked 10 or 20 years ago are no longer working, and in some corners are repelling those looking for deeper spirituality. So the question of the hour is "What now?". We need more than theories and ruminations, we need earthen practices that help us be God's people, awakened to Christ's localized mission. What Karina Kreminiski has crafted in *Urban Spirituality* is a lively and substantial response to "What now?". This book is no pre-packages, ready-to-go, plug-n-play program, instead *Urban Spirituality* is dripping with raw intelligence from the streets, spaces, and place of the neighborhood. You cannot help but have a fire sparked within as you journey through this book. Karina is pioneering and plunging headlong into a mission-shaped, Jesus-enfleshed, neighborhood-soaked future for the church. She may not realize it but she is laying our a hopeful pathway for the rest of us. Thanks for being so courageous Karina!
>   -Dan White, Jr, Author of *Church as Movement: Starting and
>   Sustaining Missional-Incarnational Communities*

Urban Spirituality is the work of a thoughtful practitioner, one for whom Christian thinking and practice are seamless. Karina's gift to us is a gentle yet passionate blend of theological insight, ministry experience and a deeply personal spirituality. As a reader I am invited into the particularities of her own neighbourhood yet empowered to return to my own with a deeper awareness of God's call to be there. Every blessing to you, Karina.

-Simon Holt, Senior Minister, Collins Street Baptist Church, Melbourne

Connect rich grounded theology, innovation that only comes with actual practice, and a robust spirituality for real life, and you have *Urban Spirituality*. This excellent book not only points hopeful new ways of being the church, it guides us into practices that could create this future. Highly recommended!

-Tim Soerens, co-author of *The New Parish*

Books focusing on a missional form of spirituality are relatively rare, so when Karina's book came out we were excited. This book does not disappoint – it is an outstanding exploration of spirituality and sustainability for people involved in tough, urban contexts. Bravo Karina!

-Alan & Debra Hirsch, Founders, Forge Mission Training Network

Table of Contents

Foreword

There are many challenges facing the church in the West, but none of them will be faced well if we simply long for a past when the church was a more significant institution, or engage the future with a loss of hope, or seek to encounter the world with strategies that are not all that relevant or helpful.

In other words, it may well be that with the increasing secularisation of the West and the further marginalisation of the faith community in the broader society, this is a time for the church to engage in deep reflection. For this to be helpful, it cannot be a journey into nostalgia. Nor at the other end of the spectrum, a wishful march towards triumphalism.

This prayerful and discerning reflection needs to be multi-dimensional. It, first of all, calls us into a renewed confidence of listening to and inhabiting the biblical narratives which carry the vision of the creator/redeemer God who enters the human fray to restore and make whole a "scarred" humanity and a "wounded" ecological world. This is the domain of re-reading scripture. This reflection, secondly, can inspire us to a new relational intentionality with the God who journeys with us. The God who draws close. The God we are to engage in worship, prayer, and reflection. This has to do with the discipline of the spiritual practices. Thirdly, this reflection may lead us to find new ways of being and forming the faith community, while at this time continuing in the long tradition of the "communion of saints" found in the church's major creeds. Here the challenge of ecclesiology awaits us. And finally, all of this may well necessitate that we find new ways of engaging our world as a sign, servant, and sacrament of the Reign of God in our midst and in our world. This is domain of a renewed missional intentionality.

It is this broad, sparkling, and invitational vision that is the heartbeat of this winsome book by the urban mission practitioner, practical theologian, and spiritual guide, Dr. Karina Kreminski. And all who long for fresh ways of encountering the Gospel, hearing the "inner voice" of the brooding Spirit, forming faith communities of welcome and hospitality, and seeing and engaging our world with the hope of the God who is ahead of us, will find this book not only inspirational but also practically helpful.

The reason for this, is, that this is an embodied book. These are not the pages of an arm-chair academic. Instead, here is the wisdom and the hopes and dreams of an urban practitioner who loves her city and neighbourhood. She knows the city's "inner gestalt," its streets, its ways, its neighbors.

Inspired by one of the most central concepts of the entire Christian story, the incarnation of the One who became one of us in radication identification, service, humiliation, and death and came to new life in resurrection power, Dr. Kreminski seeks to follow in the footsteps of One who is not called Messiah, but One who is also a bright example in the practice of incarnational mission. Jesus, through the Spirit and in the service of the faith community, can be "found" in our streets and side-walks.

All the important theological themes of Incarnation, Trinity, Redemption, and Ecclesiology spill over in this book onto the streets of Australia's major cities, carried by this unconventional missioner and her friends. In all of this, the word "playful" comes to mind, rather than the word "strategic" which we use so frequently and often so glibly. Word and Spirit at play is the grand ethos of this book.

And all of this comes to the most practical expression in the urban missional practices and spirituality that makes this book both visionary and doable.

Simmering in these pages is a renewed hope for the church and for the world.

Charles Ringma,
Emeritus Professor of Mission Studies, Regent College, Vancouver.

Introduction

Lord, help me now to unclutter my life, to organize myself in the direction of simplicity. Lord, teach me to listen to my heart; teach me to welcome change, instead of fearing it. Lord, I give you these stirrings inside me. I give you my discontent. I give you my restlessness. I give you my doubt. I give you my despair. I give you all the longings I hold inside. Help me to listen to these signs of change, of growth; help me to listen seriously and follow where they lead through the breathtaking empty space of an open door.
– Common Prayer: A Liturgy for Ordinary Pepole

There is a tension within human beings, which is that we simultaneously long for but also flee from any change in our lives. I felt this tension in my life just over two years ago when the Spirit of God whispered into my inner being the electrifying but frightening words, "Now is the time to move." I had been living in a home in a quiet suburb of Sydney and pastoring in a medium sized church for twelve years. I enjoyed those years and felt that God was training me in the skills of pastoring. Pastoring did not come naturally to me so God had some serious work to do in order to teach me the disciplines of patience, commitment to people and practicing downright ordinariness. There were some very difficult times over those years typically associated with leadership; struggles with people, difficulties with church growth, staff concerns. Overall, however, I was enjoying my life. I was comfortable. I wasn't really seeking change and yet, within me there was an emerging dissatisfaction with the status quo. Into this growing dissatisfaction spoke that voice which birthed the fresh thought in my mind of moving home and changing my job.

I felt a fear and exhilaration seeping through my body as I moved into the inner city of Sydney. Fear because I had no idea what I was doing and exhilaration because of the freedom that comes with taking a step of faith in God's direction. My aim was to start up a missional community in the city. I sensed that God was now opening up a dusty compartment within me labelled "Pioneer" which had to some extent laid dormant during my years of pastoring in an established church. As I mentioned, God had me in pastoral training school during my years leading a church and while this was a time of steep learning and filled with precious moments, it left little opportunity to explore the pioneering side of me that loves to explore, start new things and take risks. Pastoring is not all about status quo and maintenance of course; however, in my experience it was primarily a role that concerned itself around the maintenance of the church for the care of the people within the church.

The advantage of being middle aged when making such a drastic kind of change in life is that you are not in as much of a hurry as you might have been when speed was a value in former years. So, I was happy and relieved when I felt that God was saying to me that I needed to take a slow and long-term approach to developing a missional community in the inner city. I had become disillusioned with the promises of the church growth movement, critical of the way that Christianity had succumbed to the false narratives of our Western culture and fed up with the consumeristic tendencies within me, which watered down my faith. I wanted to cultivate a missional community that would emerge from the streets, spaces and places of my neighborhood rather than importing pre-packaged, ready-to-go, instant and polished products from the supermarkets of Christian culture into my neighborhood.

I wondered what it would look like to cultivate a missional community in my inner city village that would be an expression of what the missionary Spirit of God was doing in my local community. I have always loved the city and knew that I would spend the latter part of my life there. For a season, I lived in Buenos Aires and was intoxicated by the smells, sights, sounds and rhythms of a big city. When I moved back to Sydney and had to live in the suburbs, I remember feeling deflated and as though a part of me had died. I felt like I became more alive when living in urban spaces and that life in the suburbs did not sit quite right in my soul. Slowly, I began to realise that God was the author of these feelings. God was working through my desires and giving me a love for the city. God was grounding me in a context where he would send me many years later. I began to notice that the city neighbourhood was a place of God's activity even though I had usually been taught to see the city as a dark, lonely place nearly forsaken by all things sacred and good. God dwelt in the mountains, the rivers and the oceans but not in human made places known for their arrogance, I was told. So, when I moved into my inner city neighborhood,

I wanted to watch, listen to and participate with the God who invites us to join with him on mission, then with more confidence than we would ever have, sends us out to serve, love, and embody the good news of the gospel. I see this call as an adventure in the practice of an urban spirituality.

In this book, I will begin by describing the uniqueness of the urban environment and how this produces and necessitates an urban expression of spirituality. Do we have a positive theology of the city so that an urban spirituality can emerge from this place? Christians can however, be very muddle-headed about Christian spirituality so I will also explain the dilemmas associated with the term "spirituality" and particularly as this term is popularly misappropriated by many Christians. In the following chapters, I will reflect on four characteristics of an urban spirituality. In the early stages of my journey in establishing a missional community in my neighborhood, I have identified four distinctives that frame an urban spirituality, which can shape a strategy for an emerging missional community or local church. These qualities are Community, Place-making, Discernment and The Other. Each of these values has a theological undergirding. Community springs from a deeper understanding of the Trinity and the way in which we absorb the truth that we are made in the image of a Trinitarian God. I point out that the quality of Place-making has to be based on a firm understanding of the incarnation and how this impacts our daily life in our neighborhood. As we think about the characteristic of Discernment in urban spirituality, we must have a clear vision of what it means to discern the presence of the Spirit of God in our community. If we do not understand this, then we will be confused about what exactly we are listening for in order to impact our environment. Lastly, as we think about The Other, we need to understand *kenosis* or cruciformity if we are going to truly connect with and be friends with those who we might normally walk straight past on the streets of our neighborhoods.

As this book is for practitioners of the faith, I also want to map out a pathway for the embodied practice of an urban spirituality. After looking at some ancient practices of a missional spirituality in Chapter Six, I will explain the benefits of and difficulties with spiritual disciplines in Chapter Seven. Most of us are comfortable with the idea of spiritual practices for the purpose of formation into the image of Jesus. However, I want to explore what a set of missional practices would look like and how we can make these a reality in our lives so that a missional community might take shape from within our neighborhood.

This book is written at the very early and exciting stage of my journey in exploring what it looks like to facilitate a missional community in growing from the ground up, within a local community. The focus is on formation as opposed to methodology and strategy not because I do not think that those things are important, but because spiritual formation is something that we need to pay closer attention to today. We have for too long focused on quick fixes, pop up churches and strategic solutions, which have left us malnourished and emaciated, yet bloated from our over-consumption of these unsatisfying approaches. This has become quite unhealthy. My hope is that the church would go deeper rather than quicker, smaller rather than bigger and reflect on formation rather than overly relying on leadership and management techniques.

I hope you find within this book great encouragement and rest rather than yet another wearisome strategy for church growth or planting. I find that many books I read which are for practitioners, are so focused on activity that they underplay our spirituality. I believe that pioneers in urban spaces need to have an integrated faith, which simultaneously practices mission and spirituality, activity and rest, abiding and moving forward. I pray that God might place within you a mustard seed sized desire to truly love the place where you live. I pray we would then see more missional communities, more than we can count, growing quietly, steadily and with an unflinching persistence and beauty in our local neighborhoods all around the world.

Part One

Chapter One:
An Urban Spirituality for God's Missionary People

For when man is faced with a curse he answers, "I'll take care of my problems." And he puts everything to work to become powerful, to keep the curse from having its effects. He creates the arts and the sciences, he raises an army, he constructs chariots, he builds cities. The spirit of might is a response to the divine curse. - Jacques Ellul

As I sat in my local inner-city café one day writing this book, the barista came over to me and we started talking. "What are you writing?" he asked me. I told him that I was working on a book. He looked interested and his eyes lit up. He asked me what the book was about and I said urban spirituality. His eyes lit up more, "That sounds interesting. I feel like I know what urban means and also what spirituality means, but I'm not sure what those two words together mean." I smiled and told him that I was just working through the meaning of the term myself.

What Makes the Urban Context Unique?

Most of us would intuitively know the differences between urban, suburban and rural contexts, however, giving a precise definition of what it is to be urban is not as easy as it seems. The term urban is used to describe the characteristics that come with living in a city. Phillip Sheldrake defines "city" as "Urban environments characterized not simply by substantial size or large population but also by diversity-social, cultural, ethnic and religious."[1] We could perhaps see these two characteristics of size and heterogeneity as marks of a city that contribute to the development of an urban culture. A large amount of heterogeneous people concentrated in a place will result in the diversity, complexity, challenges and benefits that typically make up urban culture. Eric Jacobsen also wrestles with defining the words "city" and "urban". He says that we need a definition of the city that is broad but also specific enough to make sense of its uniqueness. Instead of limiting the definitions to statistics, population numbers or physical attributes, he says "The most meaningful way that I have found to define a city is to say that you tend to know when you are in one."[2] Even though this seems to take us back to a more intuitive framework, he fleshes out what he means by listing six distinct markers of the city, which I agree with and find helpful when it comes to reflecting on the uniqueness of the city. He lists them as public spaces, mixed-use zoning, local economy, beauty and quality in the built environment, critical mass and presence of strangers.[3]

---

[1] Phillip Sheldrake, "The Spiritual City:Theology,Spirituality and the Urban," (Chichester,West Sussex: John Wiley and Sons, 2014). Kindle Edition. Loc 2.
[2] Eric Jacobsen, "*Sidewalks in the Kingdom: New Urbanism and the Christian Faith,*" (Grand Rapids:MI: Brazos Press, 2003). Kindle. Loc 1261
[3] Ibid.

An urban spirituality needs to take into account these markers of a city that effectively shape an urban culture.

When I first moved into my inner-city neighborhood I could instantly sense I had entered a very different space to where I had been living before. As I walked the streets of my new home, everything felt closer and more concentrated. I noticed more public spaces, which encouraged me to come out of my unit more often, and welcomed me to interact in the parks and sit on the carved out patches of green grass. I saw more tourists and people movement on my street as those from outside my community came to enjoy and consume all the offerings of the city. I can even remember being shocked once when I encountered a tour group led by a guide who was eloquently sharing with a group of global visitors, about the history of my street where I lived. In fact, I can identify with most of the markers that Jacobsen mentions in his list.

The city also has a broader culture-shaping narrative that frames these markers. In other words, the urban story shapes other stories in our broader society. This story communicates to us the importance of the city and is something to keep in mind when we think about the uniqueness of the city. Tim Gorringe expresses this culture-shaping narrative well when he says, "The city is purposive in a qualitatively different way to the village or town. It represents a corporate attempt to fashion the human future. It is 'larger than life'; the buzz of its diverse trades and conditions stimulates both art and ideas."[4] The city and

---

[4] Tim Gorringe, *A Theology of the Built Environment: Justice,Empowerment,Redemption* (Cambridge: Cambridge University Press, 2002), 148.

the urban values that come with it have a broader influence on our society. This is one of the reasons that it is hard to distinguish the characteristics of urban culture. Urban culture has impacted suburban spaces and this enmeshment makes the task of discerning the delineations between urban and suburban for example, a slippery assignment. This is not to say that the rural or suburban does not impact the urban, only to say that because of some of the distinct marks of the city, this has given birth to the city as a broader culture shaping entity. Andrew Davey agrees and says

> Urban Culture is endemic in our global society. The global powers of media and communications, of economics and politics derive from cities, but there are few settlements where their impact is not felt. The cultural artefacts of the urban world move freely between city and village. Through advertising in all types of communication, the global brands of urban lifestyles captivate and create new cultures of consumption.[5]

Perhaps you are reading this book while living in suburbia but feel more like you are dwelling in an urban space sometimes. One of the reasons for this is this all-pervasive quality of urban culture. It has become part of the air we breathe. You might for example, spend a day in the city shopping and buy clothes which are designed for more "urban wear" and then you might go home to your place which is just outside the city but notice that certain cafes which usually exist in the city have now come closer to your neighborhood. As you travel into and out of the city, you see that art galleries which usually only put on exhibitions in urban places are now establishing shows out of the city. All of this; the entertainment, food culture, art, clothing and advertising impacts each of us whether we are urban dwellers or not.

---

[5] Andrew Davey, *Urban Christianity and Global Order: Theological Resources for an Urban Future* (London: SPCK, 2001), 18.

Since cities have this culture-shaping characteristic, you might imagine that they then need to have a vision themselves as they influence our broader society. I think individual cities have this capacity and responsibility to think about what kind of vision they will encapsulate and communicate to broader society and the world. Sheldrake points to Joel Kotkin's study *The City: A Global History*, which says that "Throughout history successful cities have performed three critical functions in varying ways- the provision of security, the hosting of commerce, and the creation of sacred space."[6] Moreover, Kotkin also believes that the city should itself be a sacred place that "offers an inspiring vision of human existence."[7] I agree with this vision. If cities have grand narratives that shape broader society, then there must be a spiritual element that contributes to a city's make up so that this can also impact and influence our culture. This is also why we need to recover a more positive theology of the city that will shape our spirituality and practices. At a time when we are experiencing globally the impact of urban culture more and more, Christians must reflect on the city and urbanism from God's perspective. My concern is that instead, because we have in recent times largely ignored the city and fled to the comfort of suburbia, we have become more a religion of and for the middle-class and suburban cultures in the West.

What comes to mind when you think of the city? In general, I find that many Christians have a bleak view of the city. Often when I speak with my peers in ministry about the city they tend to want to avoid doing long-term ministry there. It is perceived as a place that is unhealthy for nurturing children, a

---

[6] Sheldrake, *Spiritual City*, 4.
[7] Ibid.

context which can be dangerous, and a place that lacks community, is congested, polluted and too busy.

Four biblical images of the city capture our imagination as Christians; the tower of Babel, Nineveh, Babylon and Jerusalem. Most of these images are seen in a negative or at least a confused light. If we look at the story of Babel in Genesis 11, we notice a few things that cast a dark shadow on cities. The intention of the people of "the whole earth" (v1) was to build a city and a tower in order to "make a name for ourselves" (v4). Putting that into the context of the ancient world, this desire is an indication of a darker drive than the simple desire for acknowledgment. The parent or ancestor named a relative, so to name oneself, meant ultimately to reject and usurp the authority of that ancestor. We know the tower of Babel to be a story that symbolises pride, hubris, the "self-made" person and rebellion towards God. The story of Jonah and the city of Nineveh also brings up negative images in our minds. In Jonah 1:2 God describes the city as a "great city" but he also says, "Its wickedness has come up before me". It is a city that has inhabitants who are so confused in their thinking because of evil that "they do not know their right hand from their left" (4:11). By the time we get to the book of Revelation in the New Testament, the city of Babylon becomes a metaphor for all that is evil, which stands contrary to God. Lastly, while the city of Jerusalem in the Bible is a picture of the presence of God, it has a checkered history perhaps best summarized by Jesus' sigh of exasperation, "O Jerusalem, Jerusalem, the city that kills the prophets and stones God's messengers! How often I have wanted to gather your children together as a hen

when they wrote that they want to be heavenly minded and that this is what is means to be like God. I suspect they did not mean living as a fully embodied person in the midst of the muck of this world. And I think of Amazing Grace, a beautiful hymn that contains the line "The earth will soon dissolve like snow". I also wonder if John Newton who wrote Amazing Grace had room in his theology for a restored universe in a material sense, which means that the world will actually not dissolve but rather be renewed. Some of all of this may be due to bad theology or a misinterpretation of Scripture but I do also wonder if there is a Gnosticism revealing itself to some extent that is conveying the message that the world and the flesh do not matter, only the spiritual is of importance. Biblical scholar Michael Gorman says this:

> For many people, including Christians of various kinds, the word spirituality connotes an experience of the transcendent, even specifically of God or Jesus, that is not connected to life in the world. Its purpose so to speak is to transport people out of the trials and tribulations of this world through mystical experience(s), an interiority focused on the self or the god/God within, or an eschatological orientation that pays scant if any attention to social ills...The resulting spirituality is often otherworldly, escapist and even narcissistic.[10]

Gorman is articulating here the way in which Christian spirituality has been influenced by some of the narratives of our world. Christianity has syncretised with some of these narratives to our detriment and as a result, our thinking and practice has become a distorted expression of the imitation of Jesus. I can identify four ways that we have distorted living out a Christian spirituality. Firstly, our spirituality is disembodied and "other-worldly" rather than incarnational and "this-worldly". Charles Taylor in his magnum opus *A Secular*

---

[10] Michael Gorman, "The This-Worldliness of the New Testament's Otherworldly Spirituality," in *The Bible and Spirituality* ed. J. McConville A. Lincoln, L. Pietersen (Eugene OR: Cascade, 2013), 151.

Age uses the term "excarnate" to describe the way in which our faith has become dislocated from our practice.[11] This is very evident in our Christian culture. We love our books, conferences and great sermons as Christians. However, these tools can trick us into thinking that by accessing more content, we can be transformed. How does authentic transformation happen? Not simply through attaining more knowledge. We can know perfectly well the complexities, intricacies and beauty of the gospel and yet fail to embody it. Yet we consistently put on pedestals scholars and those who have correct doctrine. In other words, we idolize knowledge and content. Of course, doctrine and intellectual pursuits are important. I teach at a theological college and value learning. However, I would argue that knowledge and correct doctrine sadly, have become the primary markers of a true Christian instead of embodied action. In fact, we tend to be suspicious of those who for example, live out their faith by radically befriending the marginalized in our communities. We even wonder if they have moved outside the boundaries of Evangelical Christianity. These people may or may not have correct doctrine yet their actions, even though they are closer to following the way of Jesus, are treated with suspicion. This disassociation between theory and practice for Christianity is disastrous. We become hearers of the word not doers, we love in word rather than in deed and action. Love however, from a Christian perspective always manifests itself in action.

Secondly, our expression of Christian spirituality has become affected by the narcissism in our world and has often become more about "self-growth" or

---

[11] Charles Taylor, *A Secular Age* (Cambridge MA: Harvard University Press, 2007), 771.

"self-actualization". Often when we think about spirituality and formation we can be very focused on our growth, our self-improvement, and our flourishing. In this sense sometimes I think that spiritual formation can have an end goal to make us more self-actualized or moral people as opposed to people who are oriented to serve our world. Sometimes we consume spiritual growth programs in the same way that we would attend self-help courses that aim to help us live our lives for the betterment of ourselves. This goes against our call to cruciformity, which is a call to allow our lives to be shaped by the cross and be an expression of the downward mobility that we see modeled by Jesus in Philippians 2:7 where Christ "empties" himself, displaying *kenosis* rather than holding on to his life. Sometimes I wonder if we should be daily practicing "crossing ourselves" as our Catholic brothers and sisters do, simply in order to remind ourselves in an embodied way, that we live moment by moment in the light of the cross of Jesus Christ. What better way would there be to remind ourselves every day that we are walking in the way of Jesus?

Thirdly, our spirituality can sometimes be more about withdrawing from the world rather than engaging with the world. If you think about what usually comes to your mind when spirituality is mentioned, most probably images of retreat, reflection, inwardness and privacy emerge as opposed to service, action, and engagement with our neighborhood. Whenever I ask people about their views on spirituality, very few will talk about service in the community.

Once I went on a spiritual retreat. It was a few days of revelling in the beauty of the Australian bush. Several others and I were guided through the practices of traditional spiritual disciplines such as Bible memorization, silence, fasting, quiet prayer and solitude. It was a wonderful time together and we all felt refreshed and rested afterwards after basking in God's love for several days. I asked the group at the end of the retreat whether this experience of retreat had made them feel more ready to engage on God's mission in the world. Everyone either said no or felt ambivalent about this. For some reason our traditional spiritual disciplines, which are valid and good, can make us turn inward rather than oriented outwards to serve our community. Missiologist David Bosch says in his book *A Spirituality of the Road*, that this withdrawal from the world perspective emphasizes a "decisive break with the world and a flight from the 'wicked city' (as seen the in classic *Pilgrims Progress*). In this model, the world is primarily seen as a threat, as a source of contagion from which the Christian must keep himself free. To be saved means, in essence, to be saved from this world, spirituality means otherworldliness."[12] This expression of Christian spirituality is obviously not conducive to forming a body of people who are called out of the world in order to be sent back into the world and join God on his mission.

Lastly, sometimes our spirituality can be individualistic rather than communal. For some reason we have latched onto the early desert fathers' and mothers' view of spirituality which is typically the picture of a solitary, spiritual figure engaging alone with the struggles of the devil, world and flesh.[13] Instead, while

---

[12] David Bosch, *A Spirituality of the Road* (Scottdale PA: Herald Press, 1979) page 12.
[13] While I realize that some would see this as a mischaracterization of the spirituality of the desert fathers' and mothers', I would maintain that in general this is a realistic portrayal of this kind of spirituality.

we can certainly learn much wisdom from the desert mothers and fathers, we need to capture a more communal expression of spirituality that followed with the emergence of ancient monastic communities and monasteries. This more communal form of spirituality seriously challenges our Western notions of individualism, independence and the worship of the narrative of the self-made person.

This pseudo-gnostic syncretistic spirituality, which is popularly perceived and practiced, has shaped us into consumeristic, individualistic, retreating, excarnate Christians. This of course hinders the community of Christ, a pilgrim people on the move with God as he continues his mission in our world. It robs us of our identity and we begin to taste like salt that has lost its flavour, which in the end is useless.

The Formation of a Missionary People

We will need a spirituality for today that is suitable for a people of God who are missionary in heart, body and mind. Rather than being formed into an inward oriented people, we will need a theology and practice that teaches us to be and also moulds us into a people who are capable of connecting with our community and navigating the changing climate of Western Christianity.

Decades ago, in the landmark book *Missional Church: A Vision for the Sending of the Church in North America,* Darrell Guder and others challenged the notion that the church in the West existed in a Christianized culture. It was a wake-up call to many Christians who assumed that they lived in a culture that was welcoming of the Christian faith:

> The Christian church finds itself in a very different place in relation to its context. Rather than occupying a central and influential place, North American Christian Churches are increasingly marginalized, so much so that in our urban areas they represent a minority movement. It is by now a truism to speak of North America as a mission field.[14]

This marginalization of the church is partly due to the end of Christendom. Christendom as a paradigm places the church firmly at the center of society. The life of the church becomes integral to the state, social life and the family. This no longer holds true. George Hunsberger in *The Church between Gospel and Culture* quotes Kennon Callahan who says:

> The day of the churched culture is over... The day has gone when the church was generally valued by the society as important to the social and moral order and when for that reason, people tended to seek out a church for themselves. We sail today in a different kind of sea...We are caught between a Constantinian Christendom that has ended and to which we cannot return and the culture's relegation of the church to the private realm.[15]

The times that we live in are certainly challenging. The church is breathing in a new and more challenging atmosphere, which requires better praxis for the space we are moving in. If the church in the West now needs to see itself as being located in a mission field, this means we cannot assume that the culture we are interacting with is Christian. If Christendom is over, then we cannot assume the privilege that we once had. Many including myself wonder whether we should have had that privilege in the first place. If the church has in the

---

[14] "Missional Church:A Vision for the Sending of the Church in North America," ed. Darrell Guder (Grand Rapids MI: Eerdmans, 1998). Kindle Edition.Kindle Edition, Loc 139.
[15] George Hunsberger, *The Church between Gospel and Culture*, ed. Craig Van Gelder and George Hunsberger (Grand Rapids MI: Baker Books, 1996), 17.

midst of this, lost its sense of identity, has become turned in on itself, then it will need to rediscover its purpose and once again set out to sail the turbulent seas of our changing culture with discernment and good navigation. This means that the people of God will need to be formed into a missionary people in order to be the light that Jesus has called them to be in their respective communities.

In essence, this is a discipleship and formational issue. It is the area of spiritual formation. For all the writing and talk around missional theology these days, there needs to be a more concentrated effort to focus on what it means to be formed and shaped into missional people. Methodology, strategies and an activism in order to change our churches are certainly to be engaged in with caution, but if we don't focus on identity, formation and transformation, then we will not see churches becoming more willing to join with God on his mission. We all know that "missional" is not primarily about doing more outreach activities in the church but rather about our identity as Christians. In other words, to be missional is to understand that our deepest identity is that we are children of God sent into the world to cooperate with the mission of God.

To be missional is about the people of God coming to terms with who they are and so what we want to see is people being formed into "sent ones" (John 20:21). That is a spiritual concern. Matters to do with identity and formation are related to spirituality rather than strategy or methodology or even primarily activity. "Who am I?" and "Who am I becoming?" are deeply spiritual questions. Therefore, mission and spirituality are co-dependents. If that is true, then we need to think about what a missional spirituality looks like that will form us into people who are equipped to cope and thrive in the midst of the liminal place that the church finds itself in today.

This missional or mission-oriented spirituality perfectly works to frame an urban spirituality needed for God's missionary leaders, pastors, church planters and disciples. This missional posture is what we need if we want to practice a spirituality that is suitable for an urban environment. We need to be much more interested in loving our cities, moving into our cities in order to bring renewal and discerning what God is up to in our cities.

So what exactly is a mission-oriented spirituality? Roger Helland and Len Hjalmarson define a spirituality that is missional as a "spirituality that forms and feeds mission. Spiritual disciplines will form us and doing the Father's work in the community will feed us"[16] Helland and Hjalmarson view missional spirituality as a way of life or a way of being in the world as Christians. They say that many leaders in churches, however, and also the people in congregations in general, have a very programmatic view of church life. As a result, the practice of Christianity has become professionalized. Strategies for ecclesiology are taken from the market; business models and assumptions of success and drivenness are implicit in the church system. They say that, instead, being the people of God has more to do with being sons and daughters of God rather than being molded by a business model. This is a point that Helland and Hjalmarson bring to our attention,

---

[16] R. Helland and L. Hjalmarson, *"Missional Spirituality: Embodying God's Love from the inside Out,"* (Downer's Grove: IVP, 2011). Kindle. Loc 237.

We long to be competent as sons and daughters, not fortressed in temple spirituality, freed to venture out on reconnaissance with Christ on mission in the wide open expanse of God's cathedral in creation and culture... we need new maps, compasses and logbooks to navigate the turbulent oceans of cultural change and liminality.[17]

The formation of a missionary people for the urban context must happen in the daily rhythms and routines of the disciples of Jesus for true transformation to occur. Our processes for formation and discipleship in Christian culture have been too programmatic, event oriented and have sadly, sucked the life out of the adventure that living in union with Christ should be. Instead, our spirituality must be integrated with mission. In his book on missional spirituality, Barry Jones agrees with this integration of the two and says, "Insisting that these two go together like breathing in and breathing out helps us overcome the potential pathologies associated with both spirituality and missionality."[18] Missional should not be another program that churches latch onto with gusto potentially burning out all its members in the process, instead it must be a way of life.

Quite often for example, people ask me what more they need to do in order to be "missional". Whenever I hear that, I fear that striving, anxiety and drivenness stemming from our Christian culture, has entered into their frame of reference. This is counter to becoming a missional Christian modelled on Jesus. Missional is more about identity and becoming rather than primarily activism and striving. A missional spirituality will always lead to action of course, but it will come from a place of resting in the person of Jesus who lives

---

[17] Ibid., Loc 275.
[18] Barry Jones, *Dwell: Life with God for the World* (Downers Grove Il: Intervarsity Press, 2014), 26.

in us. Missiologist David Bosch said, "The involvement in the world should lead to the deepening of our relationship with and dependence on God, and the deepening of this relationship should lead to increasing involvement in the world."[19] We must find a way as followers of Jesus to allow ourselves to be shaped into missionaries while we are engaging in our communities on God's mission. In that way we are formed into sent ones and also simultaneously, we impact our contexts for transformation. This is the integrated, daily spirituality that we must live if we are going to serve in the altered times we live in. Our spirituality must not be an end in itself rather, our formation must be for the sake of the world. Jeffery Greenman defines formation helpfully in this way; "Spiritual formation is our continuing response to the reality of God's grace shaping us into the likeness of Jesus Christ, through the work of the Holy Spirit, in the community of faith, for the sake of the world."[20] I think it is the aspect of "for the sake of the world" that we have missed as Christians in the expression of our spirituality. We are blessed children of God, so that we might be a blessing to our world.

Joining with God's Mission in the City: An Urban Spirituality

This missional perspective we have been briefly skimming, must then frame an urban spirituality. So then, what are the contours of an urban spirituality? This is what I will be defining in detail in the following chapters of this book but for

---

[19] Bosch, 12.

[20] Jeffrey Greenman, "Spiritual Formation in Theological Perspective," in *Life in the Spirit: Spiritual Formation in Theological Perspective*, ed. Jeffrey Greenman(Downers Grove, IL: IVP Academic, 2010), 24.

now let me point to four broad thoughts that we should keep in mind as we explore the components of an urban spirituality.

Firstly, an urban spirituality is oriented around the *missio Dei* or the mission of God. This means that the question "What is God up to in my city?" is something that we will ask continually as people who see ourselves as God's missionaries in our neighborhood. It means that we trust that God has already gone ahead of us in his plan of redemption and recreation in our community. We need to discern where the Spirit is active, and then connect with his mission. This is quite different to the usual church posture that is to seek to draw people into a church gathering in order to introduce them to the gospel. It is of course important to connect people to a church community however, in our culture of post-Christendom in the West, people are less likely to see the need to attend a church service no matter how clever our programs and events may be. Most people today in the West do not wake up on Sunday mornings and think, "That church down the road seems to have a great sermon series on marriage enrichment on at the moment. I might just pop in this morning!" Most people are not interested in attending church at all. Our culture is becoming more "unchurched" by the moment so in order to connect with people, we must go to where they are in shared spaces, discern what God is already doing and then connect, serve and bless our community. So in other words, an urban spirituality will be a mission-oriented spirituality as I have already defined it.

Secondly, an urban spirituality considers the peculiarities of the city. This means primarily that the missional Christian loves the city and sees it as a place of God's activity. Instead of viewing the city as a place that is forsaken by God, independent from God and in rebellion towards God as many Christians do, the person who loves the city will see it as a place where God is lovingly at work in order to bless the city. A Christ-follower, who loves the city because God loves the city, sees the aspects that belong to "Babylon" and the aspects that belong to the new "Jerusalem". As I indicated before, the city rather than being either Babylon, a symbol of evil or Jerusalem a perfect place of God's presence, is currently a mixture of both. The missional disciple will be able to identify which aspects of the city run contrary to God's plan of bringing beauty, justice, life and peace to our world. She or he will also be able to discern the facets of the city that are aligned to the picture of the reign of God as we see it depicted through the gospel stories which Jesus shared.

Taking into consideration the peculiarities of the city also means noting what are the differences between urban life and other contexts such as suburban or rural. As I mentioned before this is not easy to do as the definition of urban is a difficult one to pin down. However, if we keep in mind that the city does have some peculiarities which stand in contrast to other contexts while also realising that those contexts influence and are influenced by urbanity, this will help us as we think about an urban spirituality. As I describe the marks of an urban spirituality in this book, I will keep in mind the distinctions that Jacobsen makes about living in an urban context that I have already mentioned. These distinctives or "marks" are public spaces, mixed use zoning, local economy, beauty and quality in the built environment, critical mass and presence of strangers. Most people who live in urban environments could point to these as identifiable characteristics of their neighborhoods. An urban spirituality needs to emerge from the distinctiveness of the culture of the city and while that is not always a precise work, we nevertheless need to keep this uniqueness in mind. It is also important to realize that because urban culture is so pervasive, those people who are strictly speaking, not living in city environments, can also be encouraged to practice an urban spirituality. This means that urban spirituality can then be practiced quite well in contexts that are not strictly "urban".

Thirdly, an urban spirituality crafts embodied practices for missional formation. Since an urban spirituality is missional, it will have the characteristics of being grounded, embodied and for the purpose of formation of the Christian. In the same way that the church for centuries has practiced traditional spiritual disciplines, an urban spirituality will need to design practices that are missional. The urban Christian can embody these practices so that he or she fleshes out a missional spirituality in the city. As the disciple of Jesus engages in these practices, the Holy Spirit works through them to transform us into the image of Jesus. We need to regularly engage with these kinds of practices as a method for the counter formation of the church. The culture of our cities, will seek to shape us according to the false narratives of our society and so we need to counter that culture with practices designed to form us into disciples rather than consumers, servants rather than narcissists and lovers of community rather than lone rangers.

These missional practices will be for the scattered church rather than for the gathered church. We need both kinds of practices and disciplines for our walk with God. However, an urban spirituality focuses especially on practices that people engage in outside of the church gathering. These practices ought to be what we engage in as we are "on the road", at our workplaces, in our homes and places of study as well as in the public spaces in our neighborhoods.

The formation that takes place as we engage with these missional disciplines for an urban environment will then organically shape and form a community. So this means that for those who are planting churches in urban contexts or for those who love their neighborhoods and want to build a faith community there, these practices are essential. If we believe that formation and identity must override methodology in our ecclesiology, then we will take these missional practices very seriously as we seek to ask God to shape a church community in an urban space so that it can be a welcoming witness in the city. What better way is there to plant a church than to begin by engaging with communal missional practices so that people embody the mission of God in their neighborhood? We can then trust God's Spirit to move in that faith community and show us what the next step will be in our journey as church planters. This is certainly a slow approach to church planting but I think one that will bear lasting fruit, sustain the church planter in the journey and connect with people who are far from thinking about attending a church service.

Lastly, an urban spirituality seeks the well-being of the city. On the one hand, we want to practice an urban spirituality so that we are formed into disciples of Jesus on God's mission. However, practicing an urban spirituality will also always involve seeking to impact the city in a positive way. For Christians this means understanding the values of the reign of God and working to bring those values into the city. So that means that once we discern what God is doing in our environment, we work with God to bring his salvation, peace, justice, mercy and love into our communities. God is always at work building his kingdom around us and we need to connect with him to be "builders for" the kingdom which is here and now as well as not yet fully manifest.[21] An urban spirituality will never simply be about our transformation for the sake of ourselves, but it will have a goal to impact our neighborhood positively according to what God is already doing. In this way, living out an urban spirituality shapes our environment as well as ourselves.

Can you imagine a local faith community intentionally living out an urban spirituality that forms that community into missionaries and also seeks the welfare of the city? Doesn't that sound adventurous, rewarding and much less stressful than any stale church growth program? I think it does. But this journey is not for the faint hearted. It requires embracing risk, a willingness to be searched and humbled by the Spirit of God and a posture of trusting God as you step out into unknown territory. What does that look like exactly? As we keep in mind these four broad thoughts I have summarised, we can now more concretely flesh out the marks of an urban spirituality.

---

[21] NT Wright, *Surprised by Hope: Rethinking Heaven, the Resurrection and the Mission of the Church* (NYC: Harper One, 2008), 208. Wright makes a difference between building the kingdom and "building for" the kingdom. He sees the latter as a better expression because it highlights that only God can build the kingdom.

Chapter Two:
Community

One of the marvelous things about community is that it enables us to welcome and help people in a way we couldn't as individuals. When we pool our strength and share the work and responsibility, we can welcome many people, even those in deep distress, and perhaps help them find self-confidence and inner healing. - Jean Vanier

Those who love their dream of a Christian community more than they love the Christian community itself become destroyers of that Christian community even though their personal intentions may be ever so honest, earnest and sacrificial. – Dietrich Bonhoeffer

When I moved into my neighborhood, it made me think a lot about how we use the word community. On the one hand, *community* is a word that describes a geographical area and the people that live in that place. You could say then, that the word when we use it in this way is a neutral word. So for example, the community where I dwell in the inner city is in a specific village in that city in the midst of about ten or so other villages in that space. I live in a particular community in the inner city of Sydney.

However, we also use the word community to convey certain values. Often when we use the word community what we really mean to convey are values such as connectivity, respect, care and interdependence. In that sense, community is a very subjective experience. You either experience community or not, which means that you either feel connectedness with others or the opposite. You might experience isolation and discord in the midst of a group of people for instance. To most people community means having a sense of truly belonging. When we don't feel like we belong we feel unanchored, disconnected, and sometimes we can even feel as though we begin to lose our identity. Part of our identity comes from our connection and relationship with others so when we lose that, it can be very disorienting.

In my neighborhood, community is something that people deeply desire and they intentionally take steps to find it. So if I take a walk around my neighborhood I will always see people sharing a coffee in a hole-in-the-wall cafe, stopping at a local park to talk with one another as they connect through their kids or pets, attending festivals, events, markets where they can feel like they belong to something bigger and greater than themselves. Often we lament today that our value of community is breaking down or being undermined. While I agree with this statement, I also think that the desire for community is so strong in humans, that we will instinctively seek this out as well as structure our lives around this longing. There are certainly issues in my local community around alienation, loneliness and displacement. However, people intuitively resonate with the idea of community; moreover, they crave it and take intentional steps in order to connect with one another.

Thinking about community is crucial when we are describing an urban spirituality. It is important because a feature of the city and urban life is concentration of people. Usually this is one aspect that comes to mind when we think about urban life. When we think about urbanity, we visualise crowds of people, limited spaces, congestion and perhaps potential for disconnection. However, I think that this mark of a city is then an opportunity for us to practice our urban spirituality. A high concentration of people in a particular space can be an opportunity for us to work with God's Spirit present in the neighborhood we live in, to build authentic community where everyone feels welcomed.

Instead of seeing the distinctive of high population in cities as a liability, Eric Jacobsen helpfully sees it as a potential for God to work in order to build his kingdom. Jacobsen says that the difference with cities is that they have a "critical mass" of people that is crucial for connections to be made. He says, "Critical mass can be a great asset to a particular locale and in many respects is a sign of the health and prosperity of an area."[1] Instead of seeing high density as a problem, he conveys that when city planning is done well, high density can be an advantage in fostering urban culture as an incubator of creative connections, a gateway to new ideas and as patron to the arts. He argues that this can only happen when there is a critical mass of people and well-planned high density living, as opposed to overcrowding.[2]

This is a refreshing perspective because one of the reasons we have fled from cities is because of the need for space and the antipathy towards congestion.

---

[1] Jacobsen, *Sidewalks in the Kingdom* Loc2341
[2] Ibid., Loc 2301-2347

Historically the rationale behind the creation of the suburbs was to provide a utopia which countered the negative aspects of city living. While the city was dingy and dirty, suburbia was designed to be clean and sanitised. If the city was overcrowded, suburbia was created to be a place with wide-open spaces and sprawling lawns and streets so that running into too many people was unlikely. Simon Carey Holt says that although suburbia began in pre-industrial times as wastelands on the edges of cities, it "found renewal when the rich began to reclaim the rural edges as places of escape. Increasingly the impact of industrialization- overcrowding and pollution in particular- rendered city centers almost unliveable; suburbia became a lifestyle choice for those who had the means to flee."[3] You can imagine that this brand new vision was highly attractive to a post war community of people seeking peace, tranquillity and solace. Holt says, "This new suburbia embodied the hopefulness that characterised life in this post-war period. It represented financial opportunity, the sanctity of the family unit and the tranquillity and self-reliance highly valued after the chaos of the war years."[4]

Historically, we have fled the cities because of overcrowding, perceptions of uncleanliness, ungodliness and moved away to get distance, peace and personal space. Families have moved into suburbia because of factors such as greater spaces for children to play, better access to public schools and the perceived safety of suburbia compared to the city that is often seen as a context for crime.

---

[3] Simon Carey Holt, "God Next Door: Spirituality and Mission in the Neighbourhood," (Brunswick East: Acorn Press, 2007). Kindle Edition.Loc679
[4] Ibid., Loc 688

However, this has left a gap regarding Christian influence in the city. Jacobsen observes,

> Critical mass is an important but easily misunderstood feature of urban life. It has played a key role in much of the development of civilisation and much of the progress for the kingdom of God...In our attempts to avoid overcrowding and to preserve personal space; we have cut ourselves off from the rest of humanity and have severely limited the kinds of collective achievements we can make as a species.

Instead of fearing high density living, we need to embrace this as a core and helpful aspect of urban life. As Jacobsen does, we also need to see critical mass as a potential instrument that God uses to build his kingdom in urban spaces.

If we begin to see critical mass as a distinct and positive mark of urban living, this can help us to define and explore an urban spirituality. As more and more people populate a particular geographical space, the challenge and opportunity for Christians will be to work with God to create a community that welcomes everyone and recognises the worth of each individual in that shared space. So rather than fleeing community, an urban spirituality is about the development and practice of community. It counters our societal tendencies in the West towards individualism and self-absorption. If it is innate within the human heart to desire connectivity, intimacy and belonging, then an urban spirituality will work with the reality of high density living in urban spaces and join God as he builds community, which reflects the values of the reign of God among people living there. Instead of fleeing from populated spaces, more Christians must move towards them, become accustomed to them, and work with God's mission to connect with human longing in that place. Christians can visualize this kind of community because we follow a Trinitarian God who is three in one- a community

Trinitarian Christianity

Christian theology has much to say on the topic of community. The reason for this could not be more foundational or significant, which is that the God who we worship is three persons in community with one another. Moreover, humans are made in the image of this one God in three persons and so we reflect that nature of God as we live out our lives. Let's explore those two truths so that we can apply them to urban spirituality.

Often when I listen to people praying in public I very frequently hear God addressed as "Father God". This is correct of course. Jesus tells us that when we pray we are to pray to our heavenly Father (Matthew 6:9). But I sometimes wonder why I don't hear people praying to Jesus or the Holy Spirit as regularly. There are must be many reasons for this, but one possibility is that Christians still visualize God as a solitary, usually male being, removed from their lives. In other words, I think we often forget the communitarian essence of God. We hear the term Trinity and understand the concept, even though of course the Trinity defies precise explanation, but we don't think about how being Trinitarian Christians can impact our lives. Karl Rahner says

> Despite their orthodox confession of the Trinity, Christians are in their practical life almost mere "monotheists"...it is as though this mystery has been revealed for its own sake and that even after it has been made known to us it remains as a reality, locked up within itself. We make statements about it but as a reality it has nothing to do with us at all.[5]

---

[5] David Cunningham, *These Three Are One: The Practice of Trinitarian Theology* (Oxford: Blackwell, 1998), 29.

45

The nature of God, as Rahner implies in this quote, is deeply mysterious. When we venture into trying to describe the very essence of God, we know that we are on sacred ground and need a good dose of humility as we begin. Nevertheless, we can listen to scripture and tradition, which can help us to better articulate the internal dynamics of the three persons. Rather than focusing so much on the different roles of the three persons, I think that it is helpful even if thorny, to think about how the three persons in community relate to one another. The Ancients used the term *perichoresis* to describe the internal dynamics of Father, Son and Spirit. *Perichoresis* can be defined as:

> [The] mutual interdependence, even mutual interpenetration of Father, Son and Holy Spirit in their Trinitarian relation with one another. It seeks to explain the nature of the divine life with the assertion that while the three members of the trinity remain wholly distinct from each other, they are also bound together, wholly interior to each other in such a way that the Father, Son and holy Spirit are dependent on each other for their very identities as Father, Son and Holy Spirit.[6]

Seeing the Godhead in this way means that we describe the relationship between the Father, Son and Holy Spirit as interdependent, mutual, equal and self-sacrificing. The three persons share the same vision, goal and values so intimately, that we can say that we worship one God, not three. I think that we can see a glimpse of this kind of inter-dwelling and mutuality in scripture also. One example is in Luke 10:21-22, which says,

> At that same hour Jesus rejoiced in the Holy Spirit and said, "I thank you, Father, Lord of heaven and earth, because you have hidden these things from the wise and the intelligent and have revealed them to infants; yes, Father, for such was your gracious will. All things have been

---

[6] John Franke, "God Is Love," in *Trinitarian Theology for the Church*, ed. David Lauber Daniel treier(Downers Grove, IL: Intervarsity Press, 2009), 116.

handed over to me by my Father; and no one knows who the Son is except the Father, or who the Father is except the Son and anyone to whom the Son chooses to reveal him."

We get a glimpse here into the life of the three persons as Jesus rejoiced in the Spirit as he prays to the Father. We see the mutuality, shared goals and joyful life lived between the three persons.

I think that we can then say that if this is the nature of the Godhead and we have been made in the image of God, we are to somehow reflect this nature in our relationships with one another. Many people today caution the "application" of the Trinity. They argue that we are standing on sacred ground when we are discussing the internal dynamics of God and therefore fear muddying the purity of God's essence. I agree that we are standing on sacred ground as we talk about the Trinity. We also need to take care when we use words such as "persons", "relationality", and "interdependence" to describe the mystery of God. We are using loaded human terms to describe God that will never actually suffice. So this is a caution for us to keep in mind. I disagree however that we cannot connect Trinitarian understandings in some way to our everyday lives. Of course, we do need to maintain humility and caution; we can't apply the nature of God to any circumstance we wish. However, I think it is quite feasible to describe the communal nature of God as much as we can and then think about how this applies to humans who are made in God's image. Christian theology has for too long left the Trinity in a place of conceptual theology and abstraction without any application whatsoever as the quote by Rahner implied. Feminist theologian Catherine LaCugna agrees and says, "The doctrine of the Trinity properly understood is the affirmation of God's intimate communion with us through Jesus Christ in the Holy Spirit. As such, it is an eminently practical doctrine with far reaching consequences for the Christian life."[7]

Theologian Colin Gunton provocatively asks, "Suppose, then, that we begin with the hypothesis that the sole proper ontological basis for the church is the being of God, who is what he is as the communion of Father, Son and Spirit. Where does that lead us?"[8] I think this is a good question to ask of the church and I will return to that. However, I would expand his question to include all of humanity. If all of humanity is made in the image of a God who is Trinitarian then where does that lead us? One very important truth that emerges as we seek to answer that question as we discover that community, not individualism, is at the core of what it means to be a human being. This is very important for urban spirituality, which highlights relationship and community as opposed to individualism and isolation.

The West has been enamoured with the vision of a rugged individualism especially since the Enlightenment. This has championed more traditionally masculine characteristics such as highlighting the individual, marginalizing teamwork, compartmentalization and the rational over the intuitive, facts over stories. All these qualities are needed on balance however; the West has over indulged on those qualities that favour individualism rather than prizing relationship and community. So when we apply the doctrine of the Trinity,

---

[7] Cunningham, 30.
[8] Colin Gunton, *The Promise of Trinitarian Theology* (Edinburgh: T&T Clark, 1991), 71.

refreshingly, we notice that, "In many ways ...the doctrine of the Trinity leads us to see that life in its essence is relationship. While so many in our society celebrate the significance of the solitary individual, the truth is that humans are by nature and design, deeply dependent upon one another."[9] Phillip Sheldrake cautions us around the reductionism of equating the application of the trinity to mere relationality. However, he radically takes Bolsinger's assertion to the next level and states that the essence of God existing in community forever impacts the way that we define human beings. He says, "A person is not a self-contained category. Both individually and interrelationship are structured into the very nature of what it is to be human."[10] Therefore, human beings are self-defined as well as interrelated and this is core to what it means to be human. If this is true, then the church has a lot to say to the world about existing and thriving in authentic community. In fact, true Trinitarian community would then be crucial for Christians to embody in a world that is sadly, full of people experiencing existential loneliness, fragmentation and alienation.

For this reason, I think the church must itself display a deeper expression of community in our world as a witness. We are after all, a community that is modelled in some sense on the relationality of a God who is Father, Son and Holy Spirit. This is our spirituality to live as true human beings and to then show the world what it looks like to be truly human. We can offer a manifestation of community, which is counter to the false narratives of our world, shaped by reign of God values and led by a people of God who practice

---

[9] Tod Bolsinger, *It Takes a Church to Raise a Christian: How the Community of God Transforms Lives* (Grand Rapids MI: Brazos Press, 2004), 61.
[10] Sheldrake, Loc 3574.

embodied love towards others. Why are we so slow to present this to our world? Clearly, there are many churches that do community well. Maybe your church is one of those. But do we usually see churches courageously practicing the counter cultural values of the reign of God such as love of the "other", radical surrender and generous hospitality, which create Trinitarian community? Do we see the church leading in and bringing healing to our society by building true community? Not so much. Trinitarian community is crucial for the practice of an urban spirituality but we also need to be aware of the counter narratives in our cities that will try to stop us from living this out in our neighborhoods.

Individualism, Isolationism and Fragmentation

Living in high-density areas creates wonderful opportunities for the practice of an urban spirituality. However, overcrowded cities, particularly those that succumb to bad planning, are places that can also be incubators of soul-destroying symptoms such as individualism, isolationism and fragmentation.

Authors Steve Wilkens and Mark Sanford identify individualism as a "hidden" worldview in the West today, which shapes our lives. They argue that this worldview is hidden because most people don't even realise that they are adopting it as a way of life. The worldview becomes as natural as the air we breathe. They define individualism as

> The belief that the individual is the primary reality and that our understanding of the universe and lifestyle should be centred in oneself. Individualism says that my unique interests and goals should be pursued as much as possible, by whatever means deemed proper. Thus, individuals strive for autonomy and self-sufficiency,

relying on others only as they contribute to one's personal pursuits. Family, community and society are at best, secondary considerations.[11]

When I read that definition, I shudder at the thought as you do perhaps, of human beings behaving in this way. Yet there is a lot of truth in the summary that these authors make of our individualistic mindset in contemporary times.

Today it seems that the rights of the individual reign. The individual is placed before community, rights are prioritised over responsibilities and achieving personal goals is placed before surrendering to other's needs. In *Hidden Worldviews,* the authors give an example of ancient times when individualism was seen as foolish. In ancient Greece if another city-state wanted to engage in a war against them, someone would go through the streets blowing a horn in order to convey that all must congregate in the local amphitheatre. So when local citizens became aware of this, they did what was in everyone's best interests, shut down their shops, and went over to the amphitheatre to hear from the city leaders. "However, some shop owners refused to shut down, hoping to do extra business while the competitors' businesses were closed. The Greeks referred to such persons as *idiotes*, which means someone is closed up in their own world who, concerned only with personal goals, ignores the greater good."[12]

Sadly, I think that this kind of focus on the individual at the cost of care for the community is a fact today, perhaps more so than in previous times as the Wilkens and Sanford imply. Individualism exists not only in urban spaces;

---

[11] Mark L.Sanford Steve Wilkens, *Hidden Worldviews: Eight Cultural Stories That Shape Our Lives* (Downers Grove Il: IVP Academic, 2009), 27.
[12] Ibid., 30.

however, the city amplifies this mindset because of real or perceived problems of scarcity. Overcrowding, limited affordable housing, competition for places in schools, in the urban context will often mean that people will seek after their own self-interest in order to get what they desire, rather than thinking about what the community needs. Individualism mixed in with another well-practiced worldview in the West, that is, consumerism, will often mean that we commodify people and thus dehumanize them. There is nothing wrong with consuming however; "the perpetual cycle of dissatisfaction and desire with the quest to turn everything into a commodity"[13] is very problematic. In an urban context, this is disastrous as individualism and commodifying people leads to impediments towards building Trinitarian community and an increase in fragmentation.

Once community begins to break down, we experience a fragmentation of society, which leads to an increase of people experiencing isolation and loneliness. This is a serious problem in the urban context. It is not a new insight to observe that our culture today in the West is deeply fragmented; however, the city can be a place that fosters loneliness. A story recently appeared in my local newspaper that tells about a dilapidated house that has sold in my local community for over one million dollars. The inner city village that I live in is becoming more and more gentrified leading to an increasing disparity between rich and poor. Therefore, the privileged looking for a bargain, can afford to buy ridiculously expensive homes and the poor are left isolated, lonely and increasingly marginalised from the mainstream.

---

[13] Helland and Hjalmarson, *Missional Spirituality*, Loc 413.

The house that was bought for over one million dollars, it was reported, belonged to a single woman, Natalie Wood, who lived alone. She died in that home and no one knew about it. Incredibly, her dead body remained in that home for eight years until it was found. She was labelled the "Woman that Sydney forgot". One newspaper article reads

> When police found Wood on the floor by her bed in July 2011, a month before her 87th birthday, she was little more than a skeleton and a set of bright pink dentures. Animals had gnawed holes in bones still greasy and smelly. Downstairs, in the kitchen, officers found cans of instant coffee and condensed milk long since past their use-by dates.[14]

That this kind of thing can happen in a neighborhood where many houses virtually share the same walls and confined spaces is shocking. We live in cities, towns and villages in the West where it is possible for people to buy million dollar houses and yet these homes stand alongside other homes inhabited by lonely, disenfranchised and vulnerable, poor people. Usually the two groups of people never interact or meet. This is how we can have situations where a woman can be dead in her home for eight years and no one notices. There are many stories from urban contexts similar to the story about "The woman that Sydney forgot."

When I first moved into my inner city neighborhood, I heard a story that highlighted to me the fragmentation and division that existed and still do in my community. I will elaborate on this story in later chapters. I discovered that my local shopping center was named "Murder Mall". The reason for this name showed me just how difficult it is for people to understand and respect one

---

[14] http://www.smh.com.au/nsw/natalie-wood-the-woman-sydney-forgot-20140204-31ywh.html

another who live in the same community. Many members of my community, including the homeless and those who are mentally ill, frequent the shopping village. One member of the community decided that it would be amusing to take photographs of those marginalised members in demeaning postures around the shopping village. Soon an Instagram account was set up and others were also taking photographs of these members of the community. After a while, many other people in my neighbouhood realised what was happening and in order to protect the weaker members of the community, demanded that the Instagram account be taken down. I was appalled when I heard this story. It placed before me in a very confronting way, the fragmentation that existed and exists in my neighborhood. Some people in my neighborhood felt that it was funny to laugh at those who are disenfranchised in the very community where they live. These people who struggle are also members of the community who we interact with every day and who require care from us not an attitude that mocks them. I think this kind of attitude stems from a lived out narrative of individualism and consumerism which results in dehumanizing people.

Sadly, individualism, isolation, loneliness and fragmentation are factors that can exist in the urban space in a way that may not affect rural or suburban areas in the same way. The congestion, impersonal attitudes and competition that exist because of perceived scarcity can exacerbate some of the more damaging aspects of urban life. One recent invention has been the occurrence of online community through the use of social media. While I think that community in this forum is something that can be helpful and is here to stay, I also think we need to be cautious that we don't replace online community with authentic and embodied ways of relating to each other. This can only lead ultimately to increased loneliness. Sociologist Zigmunt Bauman reflects on the more unhelpful characteristics of social media and says,

> The question of identity has changed from being something you are born with to a task: you have to create your own community. But communities aren't created, and you either have one or you don't. What the social networks can create is a substitute. The difference between a community and a network is that you belong to a community, but a network belongs to you. You feel in control. You can add friends if you wish, you can delete them if you wish. You are in control of the important people to whom you relate. People feel a little better as a result, because loneliness, abandonment, is the great fear in our individualist age. But it's so easy to add or remove friends on the internet that people fail to learn the real social skills, which you need when you go to the street, when you go to your workplace, where you find lots of people who you need to enter into sensible interaction with....Social media don't teach us to dialogue because it is so easy to avoid controversy...But most people use social media not to unite, not to open their horizons wider, but on the contrary, to cut themselves a comfort zone where the only sounds they hear are the echoes of their own voice, where the only things they see are the reflections of their own face. Social media are very useful, they provide pleasure, but they are a trap.[15]

Urban Spirituality means the practice of embodied Trinitarian community. This does not mean that social networks and the like are excluded as a form of building relationships, but Christian spirituality calls us to go deeper. Trinitarian community counters some of these damaging narratives in our neighborhoods in order to cultivate transformation and hope within others and also ourselves.

Community in Practice- Hospitality and Friendship

---

[15]http://elpais.com/elpais/2016/01/19/inenglish/1453208692_424660.html

Community is what every human being longs for. Despite the existence of fragmentation, loneliness and individualism, people desire intimacy and relationship. However, Christian spirituality is often perceived as a solitary venture. As I have said, we have for too long modelled ourselves on the Dessert Mothers and Fathers who battled the flesh, devil and world on their own. Instead, we need to return to much more communal expression of spirituality.

We need to recover this communal element to our spirituality especially in the urban context. If the urban context is often a place of congestion and overcrowding which can produce loneliness and fragmentation, then we will need to practice a spirituality that counters these factors and also forms us into a people who practice Trinitarian community. We must be formed into Trinitarian Christians and simultaneously be a witness to this expression of urban spirituality in the city where God has placed us.

Community in embodied practice, contrary to our idealized dreams, is never what we expect. It is infinitely more profound and yet at the same time mundane, challenging and perplexing. So we should never idealize community and we need to recognize that it is a gift that God gives to us. Relationships and connecting with others regularly can often be a slow and trying process. But connecting and relating with others is also deeply mysterious and wonderful. We enter into sacred space when we intimately share our lives with another human being.

I think there are two practical expressions of Trinitarian community that are crucial for an urban spirituality to flourish: hospitality and friendship. If we agree that the inner being of God exhibits a *perichoretic* nature and so we see a display of mutuality, love, interdependence, equality and intimacy, we could also then see this as an expression of hospitality. Even though Father, Son and Holy Spirit are different, they show such a deep level of hospitality towards one another, that they are one. There is inclusivity in the life of the Trinity even though there are three persons in the Godhead with different roles. There is welcome, acceptance of difference and mutual respect in the inner being of God. We see that God not only displays that in the Godself, but also God extends to reach out to humanity in order to welcome and show hospitality to us. 2 Corinthians 13:13 says "The grace of the Lord Jesus Christ, the love of God and the communion of the Holy Spirit be with all of you." Here we see a benediction that is Trinitarian but also includes a welcome to humanity to participate in this blessing.

Letty Russell believes that this can then be our model as we practice Trinitarian community with each other. She says "Hospitality is the practice of God's welcome by reaching across difference to participate in God's actions bringing justice and healing to our world in crisis."[16] Russell has a very broad view of hospitality and I think that this is appropriate as we think about the expression of Trinitarian community for an urban spirituality. Hospitality is not simply about entertainment. But from a Christian perspective it must run deeper in

---

[16] J.Shannon Clarkson, Letty Russell, Kate M. Ott, *Just Hospitality: God's Welcome in a World of Difference* (Louisville: Westminster John Knox Press, 2009), 19.

that we show love, welcome and acceptance towards those who we bump into everyday in our neighborhoods. As we do this, we can bring healing, reconciliation and justice to our world through small acts of hospitality in our community.

Hospitality does not have to be expressed in monumental acts. When we hear words such as healing, reconciliation and justice, these sometimes tend to sit as abstract and large concepts in our minds. We can localise these values by practicing them in a small, yet radical way in our community. Elizabeth Newman says "If hospitality is our participation in God's giving and receiving, then as scripture testifies, this gift and reception is always particular, concrete and seemingly insignificant."[17]

A woman who was a member of the church I used to lead exemplified this one day. She would often sit at the local shopping center and watch people then pray about whatever God placed on her heart. She kept being drawn to two men who would collect all the trolleys in the shopping center. As she prayed for them regularly whenever they were working, God placed on her heart to show them hospitality and welcome. So one day during a morning tea break she bought them some baked goods to eat. Understandably, they were shocked but also pleased with the act. All she said to them was bless you. She walked back to her car and when she turned to see them, they were sitting on the trolley truck sharing the food with one another. Suddenly she got an image of the disciples breaking bread with Jesus in an act of invitation and welcome. This led her to

---

[17] Elizabeth Newman, *Untamed Hospitality* (Grand Rapids MI: Brazos Press, 2007), 174.

see these two men in a different way- with God's heart and it was an encouragement for her to keep connecting with people sharing the love of God with others in order to bless, welcome and show kindness.

Christine Pohl in her excellent book *Making Room* says

> Hospitality becomes for the Christian community a way of being the sacrament of God's love in the world, a role which certainly fits the image in Romans 12 of hospitality as an expression of our lives offered up as living sacrifices. While we might imagine sacrifice in terms of one moment of heroic martyrdom, faithful hospitality usually involves laying our lives down in little pieces, in small acts of sacrificial love and service.[18]

Small acts of kindness that show hospitality, welcome and inclusivity can be a core part of living out an urban spirituality. Rather than being a comfortable practice however, hospitality instead can be seen as a radical adventure, which brings counter the culture transformation to our community. Again, Pohl is excellent in her book as she observes that

> Although we often think of hospitality as a tame and pleasant practice, Christian hospitality has always had a subversive countercultural dimension. "Hospitality is resistance". Especially when the larger society disregards or dishonours certain persons, small acts of respect and welcome are potent far beyond themselves. They point to a different system of values and an alternate model of relationships.[19]

In the same way, that we could say hospitality is subversive and has an element of resistance to the dehumanizing and impersonal nature of the prevailing culture, friendship, is also a subversive act in the city and a display of Trinitarian community. It is a sign of the in-breaking presence of the alternate

---

[18] Christine Pohl, *Making Room: Recovering Hospitality as a Christian Tradition* (Eerdmans: Grand Rapids MI, 1999), 34.
[19] Ibid., 61.

reign of God on earth. Friendship subverts the impersonal way that our urban culture can function. These days we talk more about "building networks", "developing relationships" or "making connections". We are busy, distracted and have limited space in our lives for the time it takes to make a friend and so we become focused, project oriented and solution oriented. We want to make sure that we get some kind of benefit or advantage from the people who we are connecting with. To counter this contemporary inclination, friendship instead calls us to "personalize" and "humanize" one another. In a crowded context when we can allow fear to drive us towards demonizing, marginalizing, homogenizing, colonizing, trivializing and generalizing others who are different to us, friendship can function to disarm fear and create trust.

A helpful term to explore here is Augustine's idea of civil friendship, *amicitia*. This according to Augustine, is a friendship that "extends beyond our immediate circle to embrace all those who inhabit the same place we live in."[20] Not only does this kind of friendship include those who we live near, as opposed to the usual definition of friendship that is more about people we choose to invest in because we like them, it is also about countering our culture of pragmatism.

> As an urban ideal, *amicitia* embraces the bonds of real attachment rather than purely pragmatic arrangements or a sense of obligation. It contrasts the self-emptying Christian virtue of *caritas*, self-giving love and service. With the power- driven notion of *libido dominandi* (the lust of domination) as the driving force of an effective city.[21]

---

[20] Sheldrake, *The Spiritual City*, Loc 964.
[21] Ibid., Loc 972

We certainly need this display of friendship in the urban context. Just as God displays friendship within the three persons of the Godhead in that there is a connectivity, intimacy and valuing of each other, we must also display this as a Trinitarian community. As we do this we help humanize our city that can sometimes be an impersonal place. As I have outlined however, this is a subversive act and can be an uncomfortable process. As we learn to be friends with those who we live next to instead of those who we like because of common interests and values, this challenges the status quo and transforms us in way that we might not have expected.

Phillip Sheldrake calls this practice of friendship "urban love" and says it is challenging for various reasons. Firstly, for the reason I have mentioned in that we must befriend those who we live next door to. Secondly, we must move beyond pragmatism, utilitarianism and the language of "networking" but rather, build real attachment. Thirdly, the idea behind "urban" love is to pursue the common good. That is, the idea that we make our individual rights secondary for the sake of the good of the community[22]. The practice of hospitality and friendship is a challenge but is certainly congruent with an urban spirituality which seeks to flesh out Trinitarian community in the city. As we do this, we join with God on his mission to restore and heal our neighborhoods.

---

[22] Ibid., Loc 4690.

Chapter Three:
Place-Making

Place is indeed a protest against an unpromising pursuit of space. It is a declaration that our humanness cannot be found in escape, detachments, absence of commitment, and undefined freedom....Whereas pursuit of space may be a flight from history, a yearning for a place is a decision to enter history with an identifiable people in an identifiable pilgrimage.
- Walter Brueggemann

To inhabit a place is to dwell there in a practiced way, in a way which relies upon certain regular, trusted, habits of behaviour.
- D. Kemmis

The inner-city village where I live is an attractive place to visit. Many travellers from nearby and far away come to get an alternative view of the more popular and tourist attractions that my city has to offer. In that sense, it has become a very fashionable place to visit. People come to see the quaint, tree-lined streets and terrace houses, to get to know the history of this city and also to consume all the pleasures that the city has to offer. People pass through this little inner city village day in and day out. I used to be one of those people. I lived in the suburbs and would come to the city to consume all it had to offer, then I could go back home to the place where I lived. I was passing through, a tourist, a consumer, able to leave when I was bored, uncomfortable or didn't like what I saw. My relationship to the city was paradoxically, detached yet also idealised and romantic. All of this changed when I decided to live in this place. I started to see the city in a different light. It was now my home and neighborhood for better or worse. The question for me was; how would I choose to relate to my place?

Most people can identify with knowing the difference between simply travelling in and out of a place and settling in that place to live, making it a home. We could call the process of making the "space" that we live in a "place", place-making. William McAlpine says that "Place is more than location; it is a meaningful integration of activity and persons within location."[1] So place-making is about nurturing and developing the connectivity between our natural and built environment, relationships and activities. In that sense, it moves beyond our buildings where we live and into the neighborhood.

What sort of relationship do you have with your neighborhood? This goes further than thinking about how we treat and interact with our neighbors. We must think about our physical space, the streets we walk on, the trees, the parks, buildings, stories and events that compose our environment. Often we can have a consumerist attitude towards our neighborhood; in other words, it is a space that we use for our pleasure and to meet practical needs without thinking about how to sow into our environment where we are planted. However, a local neighborhood moves from being an abstract "space" in which we move in and out from, to a "place" where we dwell together with others, when we engage in place-making habits such as embedding ourselves in the environment, and practicing "ordinariness". For example, what has helped the space where I live become more of a place for me in my new neighborhood is

---

[1] William McAlpine, *Sacred Space for the Missional Church: Engaging Culture through the Built Environment* (Eugene: Wipf and Stock, 2011), 122.

practicing walking around my neighborhood in order to embed myself in my environment. As I walk, I feel as though I become a part of the place in which I live. It affects me and I affect my surroundings as we impact and shape one another. I love bumping into people I know at the grocery store on my walks and having very ordinary conversations that I know will ultimately deepen those friendships. I try as much as I can to do the daily stuff of life locally rather than getting into my car and driving. This means I know local shop owners and so I enjoy waving to those I know as I walk through my streets, laneways and alleys. This city strolling can also be a creative and counter cultural practice. Vivian Gornick writes in her book *The Odd Woman and the City* that the word *flaneur* was given to "the person who strolls aimlessly through the streets of the big cities in studied contrast with the hurried, purposeful activity of the crowd. It was the *flaneur*, Baudelaire thought, who would morph into the writer of the future."[2] Walking in the urban space can therefore stimulate our creativity. It can be a kind of play that we engage in and it is often in these very moments that God can speak to us by showing us for example where he is at work and how we can join with him on his mission.

The neighborhood is a unique space particularly in the urban context. Once we choose to be place-makers instead of tourists or consumers in the city, this can open up possibilities for the expression and practice of an urban spirituality. Simon Carey Holt says that the neighborhood is a place "that bridges the gap between privacy ...and the world beyond. It's not just about your experience or

---

[2] Vivian Gornick, "*The Odd Woman and the City*," (Carlton: Nero, 2015). Kindle Edition.loc 899

my experience, it's about our experience...It's an experience common to all."[3] This communal aspect of the neighborhood plays out in a peculiar way in the urban context. According to Eric Jacobsen one unique mark characteristic of urban contexts, is the abundance of public or shared spaces. So Holt rightly believes that the neighborhood is defined as a shared space and according to Jacobsen, this is even more the case in urban spaces where shared spaces are more plentiful.

Jacobsen defines public space as:

> A domain that is not controlled by an individual or a corporation, but is open for everybody to use. Sidewalks are public spaces. Benches usually are public spaces, as are parks and plazas. Public transit is a kind of public space. Streets appear to be public spaces, but for the most part we experience them from the private sphere of our cars, so they function as private spaces.[4]

Here Jacobsen contrasts suburbia to urban contexts; the former designed more for cars and the latter usually more for walking and public transport. He would argue that this design influences our experience of the place where we live. So urban contexts encourage people to walk more in their neighborhood as a result of the design and this encourages locals to connect with the built environment more deeply. Factors such as urban planning impact the city landscape and concurrently this also impacts and shapes us. This can be an opportunity or a blockage to urban spirituality.

I noticed two differences about my environment when I moved into an urban space from a suburban context. Firstly, I noticed that the streets were narrower

---

3 Holt, *The God Next Door*, Loc 404.
4 Jacobsen, *Sidewalks in the Kingdom*, Loc 1317.

and had a friendlier design for pedestrians and public transport as well as cyclists. This impacted my behaviour because it encouraged me to leave the car in the garage and take public transport or walk to local places. The more I walked in my neighborhood the more I connected to it in a grounded and engaged way, more so than if I were driving in the comfort of my sheltered car. If you think about the impact that this has on a neighborhood it can be quite significant. More people walking in my area, means more interaction with other people and therefore possibly more of a sense of community. Therefore, we impact our environment as it impacts and shapes us.

Secondly, I noticed that the space in the city is a lot more compact and congested. Cafes are smaller, laneways are tiny, gardens happen on balconies, people are closer in proximity. There is even a move towards "small-bar" culture in my city. This is very different to the sprawling spaces in suburbia. Less space means increased proximity, which means that you are more likely to bump into people frequently and encounter shared spaces more often. If your apartment is tiny then you will more likely go out to play, eat and enjoy the public spaces in the neighborhood. Again, this is an opportunity for more interaction and connection with others. Jacobsen says, "Public spaces provided the neutral territory that is necessary for the formation of informal relationships and for the building up of existing relationships. Without public spaces, it can be very difficult to develop new relationships to, in some cases, to encounter other people at all."[5] When we observe the uniqueness of the built environment in urban places, we can see plenty of opportunity to engage with

---

[5] Ibid., Loc 1322.

people, befriend people and care for the natural and built environment where God has planted us. This kind of place-making is a characteristic of urban spirituality. Jacobsen says, "One essential quality of public spaces that is relevant to Christians is the necessity of sharing when we are in a public space. Public spaces force us to think about and interact with people we don't necessarily know."[6] The local neighborhood is where we are most authentically ourselves. It is a place we can't hide because we are accountable to the people who we live next to. Often we get caught up in causes, rallies and social media activism, which can be a helpful means for bringing change to our world. However, real transformation happens as we engage with and daily bump into people in the places where we live. Then we are forced to reflect on what we must do as we encounter the other and as it personally impacts us. If I want to bring broader institutional change to our world, I must go local and get to know and love my neighbor who might be a victim of injustices such as racism, sexism and economic unfairness. The shared place of the neighborhood is the perfect place to do this.

Urban Spirituality is a spirituality that is grounded in the reality of living day-to-day life alongside other people who we might not have necessarily chosen to live next to, in close geographical proximity to each other. It is a spirituality that cares for the built environment as much as we would care for the natural environment. This is place-making. In this sense, it is a deeply incarnational spirituality. The problem is that Christian spirituality has often been expressed

---

[6] Ibid., Loc 1352.

in a disembodied way. We have also been deeply suspicious and dismissive of our built urbanscape.

Incarnational Christianity

Christianity is a deeply incarnational religion. The *missio dei* is expressed supremely through the act of God becoming human through the Son Jesus in the incarnation. The Son is sent by the Father into the world in order to redeem the world and bring restoration according to God's mission. You could say that because of God's loving nature, this leads to his practice of incarnation as a missional strategy in order to redeem the world.

The incarnation is expressed most radically and succinctly in John 1:14: "the Word became flesh and lived among us, and we have seen his glory." The expression that the "Word became flesh" is uncompromising in its declaration about the strategy that God took in order to communicate with his world. In this act, God gave up the privilege that belonged to him and lowered himself to the status of a human being in order to connect with the world. D. A Carson points to the finality of the declaration of this verse and says, "If the evangelist had only said that the eternal Word assumed manhood or adopted the form of a body, the reader steeped in the popular dualism of the Hellenistic world might have missed the point. But John is unambiguous, almost shocking in the expression he uses: the Word became flesh."[7]

---

[7] Don Carson, *The Gospel According to John* (Grand Rapids: Eerdmans, 1991), 126.

This incarnational act is made even more intimate and personal through the phrase "lived among us". The Greek word here is *skenoo*, which means 'to pitch a tent'. This reminds us of the time that Israel was wandering in the desert and the place to meet God was in the tabernacle before the temple was built. In Exodus 25:8, God commands, "Then have them make a sanctuary for me and I will dwell among them". In John 1:14, God is conveying that not only does he become a servant by engaging in the act of incarnation, but he also engages with humanity in an even more personal way; that is, by 'dwelling' with humanity. Eugene Peterson puts this poetically in *The Message* translation: "The Word became flesh and blood and moved into our neighborhood." This act of God entering human existence is a central and crucial theme in Christianity that cannot be overstated. C. S. Lewis says it directly, "The central miracle asserted by Christians is the incarnation. They say that God became man. Every other miracle prepares for this, or exhibits this, or results from this."[8]

God not only connected with our world but he did so in a very intimate way, he became human, lived among us. "God is with us" is a profound statement to make and one that when embodied, reorients us to love our neighbor who is made in the image of God and our neighborhood, the sacred space of God's missionary activity. Grasping this truth has two consequences. Firstly, we will be uncomfortable with the thought of the gospel as a mere abstract concept. The gospel must never sit in our minds as a mere concept but must be lived out. Instead, we will primarily be thinking about how the gospel can be fleshed out

---

[8] C.S Lewis, *Miracles* (New York: Macmillan, 1947), 112.

in our lives and community. Darrell Guder makes an excellent and stark point when he says

> The centrality of the community to the gospel means that the message is never disembodied. The word must always become flesh, embodied in the life of the called community. The gospel cannot be captured adequately in propositions, or creeds or theological systems...the gospel dwells in and shapes the people who are called to be its witness. The message is inextricably linked with its messengers. If there is good news in the world, then it is demonstrably good in the way that it is lived out by the community called into its service. The early church in Jerusalem lived in such a way that they had 'the goodwill of all the people' (Acts 2:47).[9]

As Christians practice an ethic of embodied love that stems from a robust incarnational theology, we become Christ's hands and feet to a watching world. The problem here of course, as we have already mentioned is that we feel more comfortable in the realm of the abstract rather than in concrete practice. We prefer to discuss ideas rather than flesh out costly, embodied love in our community. However, the Incarnation calls us to follow in the footsteps of our Lord and ground our rhetoric in practice.

Secondly, if we absorb the truth and consequences of the incarnation fully, we will see everything in our world as sacred. In other words, this means that nothing is profane but instead everything in our world is a forum for the presence, redemptive activity and beauty of God to be discovered. Again, however, this is often not the instinct of Western Christianity. Our Gnostic influenced spirituality has manifested in the prioritization of "spiritual" things

---

[9] Darrell Guder, *Incarnation and the Church's Witness* (Harrisburg: Trinity Press International, 1999).

and a distaste for earthly materials and goods. Roger Helland and Len Hjalmarson say

> Christians today regularly refer to their culture as the secular world. It's where one holds a secular job, attends a secular university, listens to secular music and watches secular movies and TV. Even though all cultures express religion and spirituality in one form or another, the so-called secular world is often wrongly perceived as a separate realm disenchanted from the sacred realm where the God way up there and Christian faith reside. Some Christians place culture in one realm and place the institutional church, Christian faith and their personal spiritual life in another realm. This dualism is secularization. [10]

This separation of sacred and secular has meant that Christians tend to focus less on the built environment as a place of God's presence and activity. That space is relegated to the secular or profane. Notably, this also has to do with our eschatology. What are our thoughts around the consummation of all things? If we believe that the world will in the end times be destroyed by God rather than restored and if we as a result live out an "escape from the world" theology, we will not be interested in our buildings, land or neighborhoods.

This is certainly something to think about when it comes to an urban spirituality because we have said that public spaces are a defining mark of the cityscape. However, if we believe that God will destroy the world at the end of time, why would we want to sow into our spaces and environment? Why would we even think that God's spirit is actively on mission there? Scholar Paula Gooder referring to the traces of Gnosticism in Christianity says

> This attitude manifests itself as a general uncertainly about a Christian attitude to anything that falls under the heading "physical". An interesting example of this might be attitudes to the environment. For

---

[10] Helland and Hjalmarson, Loc 331.

many years ,... Christians have displayed an ambivalence to creation and the environmental disaster that is approaching with ever-growing rapidity. This ambivalence emerges at least in part, out of an emphasis on the "good" of the spiritual to the exclusion of the physical. If we believe that our ultimate fate is a spiritual existence in heaven with God and that the physical world is coming to an end then it is much harder to feel motivated to act for the good of the planet.[11]

I would apply this thought to the local inner-city neighborhood and ask myself: Do I believe that my local inner city village is a place where God is at work to redeem not only the people, but also the land, buildings and community? If God is at work to reconcile all things in Christ, does this include my physical neighborhood? I would even boldly ask; which aspects of my neighborhood will I see in the new creation? We should ask ourselves these kinds of questions about the community in which God has placed us in order to challenge any dualism and unchristian Gnosticism within us that is skewing the radically incarnational nature of our faith.

Thankfully, many scholars and practitioners are increasingly focusing more on the intersection between spirituality and the built environment by developing a theology of place. Terrance Goringe writes that our Augustinian heritage has influenced us to believe that the "true Christ of history" tells us to "turn away from the preoccupations of human society", our ancient spiritual fathers encouraged us to "disentangle (ourselves) from all things created", and architects of the past wanted to evoke a sense of the "unearthly" in their buildings. All of this leads to a very displaced and disembodied view of our geography. Therefore, we must today rediscover a more positive approach to a

---

[11] Paula Gooder, *Body: Biblical Spirituality for the Whole Person* (London: SPCK, 2016), 4.

theology of the built environment.[12] Again, this impacts an urban spirituality because of the focus on public places and the built environment in cities. Cities are built, shaped and designed according to ideologies. Do we ignore this built environment as a space that is secular and fading away as we sing "turn our eyes upon Jesus" who makes the "things of the earth grow strangely dim"? Or do we input and shape our inner city neighborhoods with reign of God values? These are crucial considerations for the practice of an urban spirituality.

Once we start thinking about our built environment as just as spiritual as natural landscapes and also important in the framework of God's renewal of all things, this impacts the way that we think about the shape of our cities. Sheldrake says, "In urban environments we cannot separate functional, ethical and spiritual questions. If a city is to be more than merely efficient, it needs to embrace some sacred quality- above all it must affirm and promote the sacredness of people and the human capacity for transcendence."[13] An urban spirituality will seek to actively build an urban environment that will promote sacred spaces, compassion and respect for humanity. Cities can be impersonal, inhumane and places of fragmentation, an urban spirituality will seek to encourage values that are in line with the kingdom of God. This will happen as we who live in the city take more of an interest in things such as urban planning, local politics and environmental care. There are however, factors in the urban space that impede this kind of grounded practice of an incarnational spirituality.

---

[12] Gorringe, 9,10.
[13] Sheldrake, Loc 3121.

Transience, Displacement and Excarnation

The subtle Gnosticism, dualism, bad eschatology and suspicion of all things physical in our faith today, work against the practice of a more incarnational expression of Christianity in an urban spirituality. However, it is not only theology that is an influencer, but also cultural and societal factors come into play. Looking more broadly to our culture, there are factors which exist that work against place-making in an urban context.

We live in a time when more than ever people are much more mobile and on the move. Whereas in previous times values like stability and rootedness were enshrined in Western culture, today our world is much more transient. It could be that technology which is enabling us to travel faster, connect more quickly and have better access to information whenever we want it, is shaping us into a more distracted and impatient people. Or it may be that we are living in times when issues such as global migration, unemployment and national violence is causing increasing movement, mobility and so people are travelling to seek better opportunities.

Whatever the reasons behind our emerging tendency towards preferring transience, we have become a restless people who struggle to remain in one place long enough to develop a relationship with the physical space and the people in that community. Elie Wiesel said that the twentieth century was the "age of the expatriate, the refugee, the stateless- and the wanderer".[14] If we think about the twenty first century, we could say that this description fits even more so now. This often crushing and painful sense of disorientation felt by many people today is captured well by Brian Walsh and Steven Bouma-Prediger when they conclude, "Whether we examine the forced migrations of people who have been chased out of their homes by ethnic violence, waves of immigrants seeking economic security, the marginality of the poor in the inner city, or the placeless and lonely anonymity of the elite business class, there is a profound sense that we are all strangers."[15] This experience of disorientation or "strangeness" comes partly from an overly romantic notion of the pilgrim, the wanderer and the nomad who has no place to rest. In novelist Tash Aw's short story *Sail*, the two main characters convey a sense of displacement as they live their lives as foreigners in China. Even though Yanzu is Chinese he feels like he does not belong in his own country and Liz, the English teacher living there finds a liberating sense of abandonment and freedom in her nomadic lifestyle. Aw writes about Liz

> She loved the feeling of being between places, of being nowhere. It made her feel she could go anywhere she wanted, on her own. She would never be pinned down; she would always be her own woman, never dependent on anyone. Being on that yacht had made her realize she would always hate a sedentary life. Sedentary, it means um staying in one place, inactive, boring, that sort of thing. She could never stay anywhere, to be with anyone for too long. She wanted constant adventure, moving from one place to another.[16]

---

[14] Elie Wiesel, "Longing for Home," in *The Longing for Home*, ed. L S Rouner(Notre Dame Indiana: University of Notre Dame Press, 1996), 19.
[15] Brian Walsh S Bouma-Prediger, *Beyond Homelessness: Christian Faith in a Culture of Displacement* (Grand Rapids: Eerdmans, 2008), 8.
[16] Tash Aw, "Sail," *A Public Space*, no. 13 Summer (2011): 142.

This romantic notion of living "free" and unbound by all the constraints of stability, place and being grounded, is something that we can discern in our culture today. To be stable is boring, but to be the eternal wanderer is an ideal way of living our lives. This possibly also translates to our spirituality, which has focused much more on a spirituality of restlessness, pilgrimage, movement and seeking as opposed to a spirituality of stability, incarnation and dwelling.[17] But in reality, this romantic ideal only increases a sense of loneliness and displacement in our society and robs us of the place-making, which strengthens communities and relationships in a neighborhood. Phillip Langdon writes

> Repeated millions of times, the decision to move out robs communities of their memories and their social relationships. It leaves them shallow rooted, ill-equipped to provided their residents with sustenance during hard times. Sociologists have discovered that long-time residents make a disproportionately large contribution to a community. "Any human relationships takes time for seasons, for testing, for the kind of slow, casual knitting that will not break apart under the first signs of strain", John Killinger writes. Rapid mobility...does not afford the kind of time-years and years of time- that are necessary to become rooted in a place, to really know the neighbours, to truly belong to the community, to celebrate the great milestones of life that can be celebrated in a home church or synagogue, to feel deeply and responsibly, that there is a bond between ourselves and the land, ourselves and the house, ourselves and the neighbourhood, that nourishes and replenishes our beings.[18]

During my time living in the city, I have worked hard at building connections but more importantly, friendships in my neighborhood. However, what makes this difficult is the constant and rapid movement of people in and out of the community. Mostly, the people who I know move in order to find better jobs and take the success-laden opportunities that are offered to them. This is

---

[17] S Bouma-Prediger, Beyond Homlessness, 272.
[18] Phillip Langdon, *A Better Place to Live* (Amherst: University of Massachusetts Press, 1994), 76.

understandable, but what is the cost to our neighborhoods when we enshrine this perception of progress as a value? This romantic ideal of the nomadic lifestyle serves to impede a sense of community that can only be nurtured over time and in close proximity.

This culture of transience is also fostered in the context of our global capitalist and consumeristic world where the idea of stability is seen as unambitious. In contrast, movement, travel and displacement are seen as signs of power, privilege and ambition. This idealizes and reinforces the myth of progress. Kennesson says that this attitude of impermanence is reinforced through advertising and our innate but sometimes misplaced, searching for something better. He says

> We are in short, encouraged to be deeply committed to being uncommitted. Although most of us learned at an early age that contrary to popular belief the grass is not always greener on the other side our lives continue to embody this sentiment in countless ways. Rather than sticking with anything for any length of time- whether it be spouses, church, friends or hobbies-we tend to flit from one thing to the next in search of that missing something. As a result, convictions and practices of faithfulness and commitment rarely get the chance to sprout let alone thrive.[19]

It seems that this way of thinking has a lot of traction in our culture. Often during discussions with my peers about ministry in church, they will ruminate on that about the transient neighborhoods they live in. In the past, perhaps only some places would have said that they housed "transient" communities, however, today it seems that this way of being is the norm. My neighborhood

---

[19] Phillip Kenneson, *Life on the Vine: Cultivating the Fruit of the Spirit in Chrisitan Community* (Downer's Grove: Intervarsity Press, 1999), 185-186.

where I live in the inner city is also transient. Young adults come and go according to study and work needs. Families from other parts of the world move in for three to five years because of job opportunities. The homeless move around throughout the various villages. The inner city is known to be a place where people move about a lot, coming and going according to seasons of life, wants, perceived needs and always on the search for that "something" that is missing in life. Whenever I talk with some of my peers in ministry about place, location, and commitment to neighborhood, many think that this is an impossible ideal and that no one thinks in terms of permanence anymore. They feel that we should swim with the tide that points to increasing globalisation, online connectivity, movement and a seeking spirituality that is always on the move with a God who is always on the move. But this is perhaps to align too closely with consumerism and what is essentially a culture of capitalism.

All of this is not to say that seeking, movement and mobility are innately wrong things to practice. I don't want to idealize permanence and community either. Neighborhoods are places of tension; they can become inward looking and ghettos, homogenous compartments that do not welcome those who are different to the dominant subculture. So there are problems and risks associated with community also. However, the fact is that people today do long for community, they long for places, which are neighborhoods that foster strong relationships and physical spaces designed to be used and treasured by the whole community. Hugh Mackay in his book *What makes people Tick* notices this and says

> If you are ever tempted by the thought that contemporary Western culture is more individualistic than in the past just take a look around

you. From the family to the workplace, from the school gate to the local coffee shop or pub, and form religious, political or sporting affiliations to friendship circles, both online and offline, we are as socially interdependent as ever. Our default position as humans is together even for those of us who also cherish time alone.[20]

This is not a nostalgic longing for the past, only a recognition that we have lost the important values of place-making, community and relationships because of our obsession with and acquiescence to mobility, pilgrimage and a nomadic lifestyle.

This displacement and transience has cultivated a disembodied and excarnate way of existence that we are becoming all too comfortable with. Charles Taylor in *A Secular Age* said

> We have moved from an era in which religious life was more "embodied", where the presence of the sacred could be enacted in ritual, or seen, felt, touched, walked towards (in pilgrimage); into one which is more "in the mind", where the link with God passes more through our endorsing contested interpretations- for instance, of our political identity as religiously defined, or of God as the authority and moral source underpinning our ethical life.[21]

This excarnation is reflected more broadly in our culture with the increase of online community and less face-to-face interaction with people. Again, social media can be a positive space for community and can supplement embodied interaction; however, we are missing out when we allow online activity to be greater than connection with face-to-face relationships. People are discovering this now as they seek places to meet with one another and connect in a physical sense. One trend that is emerging in Sydney is the practice of meeting up with

---

[20] Hugh Mackay, *What Makes Us Tick? The Ten Desires That Drive Us* (Sydney: Hachette, 2010), 151.
[21] Taylor, *A Secular Age, 554.*

total strangers and looking into one another's eyes in order to establish connection. One practitioner says, "We're in a society where people are so focused on their phones and we forget to look at each other, which is really sad and it sounds really stupid... for the betterment of humanity we need to look at each other".[22] Such "spiritual practices" are becoming common in inner city neighborhoods where the values of displacement, transience, excarnation exist alongside a deep longing for intimacy, community and place-making.

Stubborn Faithfulness (Home), Embodied Love and Place-making

The Christian community has a lot to contribute in this culture where displacement, homelessness and excarnation thrive. We can engage in an incarnational spirituality that fosters faithfulness, embodiment and place-making. This spirituality can thrive in and contribute to an urban context so that we join with God on his mission to restore our neighborhoods.

As I have mentioned before, not only is our culture transient, transience is actively encouraged. Being a global citizen is worn as a badge of honour but being settled in a particular place is seen as mundane and unexciting. When I share with people my story of moving from one place to an inner city community in order to live and minister there long term, and by long term I mean decades, people tell me how bold and counter-cultural I am. It is acceptable in Christian circles to make a commitment to a person for life but

[22] http://www.abc.net.au/triplej/programs/hack/why-strangers-in-parks-are-gazing-into-each-other's-eyes/7630342

not to a place. Instead, we move from one town to another, one state to another and from one country to another based on pragmatic reasons like job opportunities, better schools and environments that are more pleasing. Yet this produces a sense of displacement within us. Many single people especially, who I know, have accepted the cultural narrative of the global citizen and move about from city to city regularly but then wonder why they have feelings of loneliness. I share with them my thoughts about being grounded in a place, which can contribute to feeling connected and as though they belong somewhere. Usually there is a glimmer of recognition around this thought however; often the "global citizen" narrative and our Western views of what constitutes "freedom" remain present and strong, overwhelming the possibility of practicing faithfulness and incarnation in a particular neighborhood.

People today are more likely to move due to job opportunities, career advancements and lifestyle choices. This changes our way of thinking about community and building relationships so that the moment we begin to plant ourselves in a community we are mentally preparing to leave again in the not too distant future. Instead of having the perspective of committing to people in our local contexts, we don't bother connecting deeply, because we know the friendships will end nearly as soon as they start as we move to the next geographical location. Sometimes movement is unavoidable and necessary in the life stages of a family. However, other times decisions could be made to remain planted in a local context, meaning perhaps sacrificing some comforts and conveniences but it may also mean being rewarded with life-long relationships and earning trust with the local community.

An urban spirituality actively counters our transient culture and practices stubborn faithfulness to a place. In essence, this is to practice the discipline of home- making. Everyone has a longing for home, a place which is familiar to us and that tells the story of our lives. To be homeless is not only to not have shelter though that is terrible enough; it is to not have a place that is familiar and an expression of who we are. Christians know that a restored universe is their ultimate home. Revelation 21:3 says "See the home of God is among mortals..." and it goes on to describe a little of what the new creation will be like. However, God has placed us in particular geographical spaces now that we must take care of, share and embody the story of the reign of God welcoming others to join us. God spoke to the exiles in Babylon these words "But seek the welfare of the city where I have sent you into exile, and pray to the Lord on its behalf, for in its welfare you will find your welfare" (Jeremiah 29:7). As we who have made our home in Christ live out our "exile" here on earth, we are to seek the peace, justice and salvation of the cities where we dwell today.

Many Christians are discovering the beauty of this urban spirituality practice. In *The Gospel after Christendom* in a chapter about exilic practices, Dwight Friesen tells the story of Pastor Paul who leads a church in Tacoma. The membership requirement of this church is that people must live and work within 15 blocks of the area of the city. This has grounded the church locally as they participate in caring for the natural and built environment. It has connected them deeply to each other and the broader community. They have found that "living, working and worshipping in close proximity strengthens

Christians missional identity formation because the people who are part of the church see one another and are seen by one another in multiple settings every week...they are finding that proximity is a crucible for formation."[23] Practicing stubborn faithfulness to a place can yield relationships grounded in trust, which can bring the right to speak into people's lives at appropriate moments. As our lives intertwine and we rely on each other, we create a web of support in the midst of a context that exhibits displacement rather than faithfulness and loyalty. This is crucial for an urban context where the sense of loneliness, displacement and disembodiment can be even more pronounced. This is not to say that practicing stability and faithfulness is easy. We might even feel as though as we practice this that the world is passing us by, we might have to give up on exciting job opportunities or we might experience frustration at the slow pace of change. I believe however, that this is partly what it means to live a counter-cultural life in the reign of God today.

Practicing incarnational spirituality in urban places keeps us accountable to embodying love in our neighborhoods. Daniel Kemmis says this practice of neighbourliness means engaging in the homely practice of being good neighbours, and keeps us accountable to actually living out what we believe and aspire to become as humans.

> Deep-seated attachment to the virtue of neighbourliness is an important but largely ignored civic asset. It is in being good neighbours that people very often engage in those simple, homely practices which are the last and best hope for revival of a genuine public life... Places have a way of

---

[23] Dwight Friesen, "Formation in the Post-Christendom Era: Exilic Practices and Missional Identity," in *The Gospel after Christendom: New Voices, New Cultures, New Expressions*, ed. Ryan Bolger(Grand Rapids: Baker Publishing, 2012), 202.

claiming people. When they claim very diverse kinds of people, those people must eventually learn to live with each other; they must learn to inhabit their place together, which they can only do through the development of certain practices of inhabitation.[24]

Sheldrake agrees with this thought about practicing the abstract in local and concrete ways linking this to a theology of incarnation. He says that thinking about place means recognising the importance of the particular rather than the universal. However, Western culture has stressed "the objective rather than the particular of the vernacular, the universal or disengaged rather than the personal and the contextual", this runs counter to the belief in, and practice of the incarnation since God himself practiced particularity, embodiment and being personal.[25]

Once we start living this out in our daily lives it means that very simple practices such as knowing our neighbors names can be a very humanising act in a context that can be dehumanising. The authors of *The Art of Neighboring* notice this point of living out what we believe in a concrete way. They say that we have not taken the commandment to love our neighbour literally enough. Rather than seeing our neighbour as the person across the other side of the world who is suffering, what about those who live next door to us? They say,

> The problem is that we have turned this simple idea into a nice saying. We put it on bumper stickers and t-shirts and go on with our lives without actually putting it into practice. But the fact is Jesus has given us a practical plan that we can actually put into practice, a plan that has the potential to change the world. The reality is though, that the

[24] Daniel Kemmis, *Community and the Politics of Place* (Norman Oklahoma: University of Oklahoma Press, 1990), 119.
[25] Sheldrake, Spiritual City, Loc 2990.

majority of Christians don't even know the names of most of their neighbors.[26]

Practicing an urban spirituality grounded in the practices of incarnational Christianity is also about place-making. Since the city is a place of a numerous amount of public spaces, place-making can be something that we practice as an expression of our spirituality. What does it look like for Christians to get involved with local councils and present a spiritual vision of the neighborhood in which they live for the betterment of that place?

Once we accept that we live in post-Christendom times and so the church building is no longer the organizing principle in a neighborhood, this will liberate us to see the broader neighborhood as a context of intertwined relationships that Christians are a part of and can contribute to. The place that God has put us in must be stewarded by Christians in its entirety. This means thinking about how the story of the reign of God is expressed through the buildings, the parks, the streets, shops and broader ecology of the neighborhood. As we engage in the urban spirituality practices of stubborn faithfulness, embodiment and place-making, we will see the story of the reign and mission of God emerging right at our doorsteps and on our streets. Let's take a short pause and think about what this story of God's rule is all about exactly.

---

[26]Dave Runyon Jay Pathak, "The Art of Neighboring: Building Genuine Relationships Right Outside Your Door," (Grand Rapids: Baker Publishing, 2012). Kindle Edition.Loc 156.

Interlude:
The Story of the Reign of God

"It helps, now and then, to step back and take the long view. The Kingdom is not only beyond our efforts: it is beyond our vision. We accomplish in our lifetime only a tiny fraction of the magnificent enterprise that is the Lord's work. Nothing we do is complete, which is another way of saying that the Kingdom always lies beyond us. No sermon says all that should be said. No prayer fully expresses our faith. No confession brings perfection. No pastoral visit brings wholeness. No program accomplishes the Church's mission. No set of goals and objectives includes everything. That is what we are about. We plant the seeds that one day will grow. We water seeds already planted knowing they hold future promise. We lay foundations that will need further development. We provide yeast that affects far beyond our capabilities. We cannot do everything and there is a sense of liberation in realizing that. This enables us to do something, and to do it very, very well. It may be incomplete, but it is a beginning, a step along the way, an opportunity for the Lord's grace to enter and do the rest. We may never see the end results, but that is the difference between the Master Builder and the worker. We are workers, not master builders; ministers, not messiahs. We are prophets of a future that is not our own." ~ attributed to Oscar Romero

We are shaped by the stories that we believe in. It is not so much the abstract truths and principles that form us, but instead it is the stories and narratives that mold us into the people who we are today. As we hear the stories which inspire us and captivate our imaginations, we are then motivated to live them out. When we see truth and courage represented through a person's story in a movie for instance, we are more likely to be inspired to action. I think this is

why Jesus told stories. When I read the story of the Good Samaritan, I marvel

at the kindness he shows and I want to emulate that in my life. Stanley

Hauerwas puts this well when he says,

> Our character is the result of our sustained attention to the world that
> gives coherence by the stories through which we have learned to form
> the story of our lives. To be moral persons is to allow stories to be told
> through us so that our manifold activities gain a coherence that allows
> us to claim them for our own...Our character is constituted by the rules,
> metaphors and stories that are combined to give a design and unity to
> the variety of things we must and must not do in our lives. If our lives
> are to be reflective and coherent our vision must be ordered around
> dominant metaphors or stories.[1]

Therefore, how we live our lives is a reflection of the stories that we have

adopted and which have adopted us. Not only that, we have personal narratives,

but what I think is also interesting is to look at the cultural narratives that

shape and form us. Tim Foster explains that,

> A cultural narrative is a story shared by others who belong to the same
> culture, subculture or tribe. It is not a linear account that moves
> coherently through successive episodes towards a climax and conclusion
> like a novel. There is nothing linear about a cultural narrative. Nor is it
> written down, but it is found hidden beneath a multiplicity of symbols,
> myths and rituals. It is told through the myths found in books,
> magazines, films, advertising, blogs and anecdotes. It is symbolized in
> fashion brands, technology, art, music and architecture. It is ritualized
> in the practices that govern each day, week and year. It is embodies in
> the values, pronouncements and lifestyle of our heroes and celebrities.
> In countless ways and from the earliest age our cultural narrative is told,
> and it is absorbed.[2]

---

[1] Stanley Hauerwas, *Vision and Virtue* (Notre Dame IN: Fides Publications, 1974), 74.
[2] Tim Foster, "The Suburban Captivity of the Church: Contextualising the Gospel for Post-Christian Australia " (Moreland VIC: Acorn Press, 2014). Kindle Edition. Loc 524.

Discerning cultural narratives is not an exact science; however, it is possible to identify them in our lives and communities. The question is then; which story are you living? What cultural narrative are you embodying day to day? Answering that question is not simple because there are many stories that exist in our culture that compete with each other. We can be living out various stories or narratives at the same time. One narrative that is common to the West for instance, is the vision of the good life. This is a narrative that many of us embody which takes hold of us, shaping us into the kinds of people who develop habits that reinforce the vision. The good life is a picture of a utopian image that we can carry which reveals what matters to us in the West. Usually it involves a good education, marriage, purchasing a home, having the right amount of children, being able to keep a good job that will pay for all of this so that we can retire to a quiet place somewhere to take care of the many grandchildren. Most of us gravitate towards and long for this story. Most of us do everything that we can to live out this story and we become disoriented and perhaps even suffer with a kind of social anxiety if this story is frustrated.

Social researcher Hugh Mackay has elaborated on our desire to live the story of "The Good Life". In a book with the same title, he points to the perception in the West that we are living in a golden age; we have access to online shopping at our command, international air travel in easier than ever, access to reliable and fuel-efficient cars and an overload of technology and information at our fingertips.[3] However, he also believes that this has caused us to create a utopian

---

[3] Hugh Mackay, *The Good Life* (Sydney: Macmillan, 2013).

vision that can insulate us from hearing the voices of those near and far who are struggling. He says

> And yet, the more you examine our Utopian fantasies and our energetic attempts to turn them into reality, the more you wonder if the very things we're so desperate to acquire as symbols of this imagined good life may be insulating us from deeper and more enduring satisfactions, fuelling our dreams while limiting our vision, encouraging us to settle for the most trivial and fleeting meanings of 'good'. Our teeth should remain perfectly bright, white and, of course, straight, regardless of their age. If we are female, we ought to have perfectly formed or re-formed breasts that resist the sagging once thought to be a natural consequence of breastfeeding and the passage of time. We should be able to track down the perfect latte, the perfect investment vehicle (perfectly safe but astonishingly lucrative) and the perfect movie (uplifting, funny, sexy *and* memorable).[4]

The narratives that we live by are not neutral and they need to be intentionally examined because, as Hauerwas points out, our character is shaped by the stories that we live. If we are living a story which is mostly about our satisfaction, comfort and prosperity, as is the case with the Western "good life" narrative, then we might be missing out on embodying a more enriching and fulfilling narrative that will help us live our lives in a way that is more in alignment with who we have been created to be. Some of the stories that we live can express a false narrative and even a destructive one. Think of the person who believes that the best way to live is to be "free" from any perceived constraints and commitments. The "global citizen" that I have mentioned previously can fit into this category. This person might live their life without any commitments to place or people; however, that may lead to loneliness. Which story leads us to life? Which story can help us to become the people who

---

[4] Ibid.

we long to be? I think the story of the reign or kingdom of God answers those kinds of questions.

We hear a lot of talk today about the reign or kingdom of God, which is a good thing because Jesus talked about this kingdom frequently in the Gospels. However, often I find that when I ask Christians simple questions like "What do you think the kingdom is?" or "What does the kingdom of God mean for you?" answers become very vague and ambiguous. Yet this story is the one we are called to live out and it is *the* Story which answers meaning of life questions such as "Who am I?" "How must I behave on this earth?" "Where am I going?"

The story of the kingdom or reign of God is the story of an alternate reality, different to the world as we see it today. It is a place where God's perfect reign is manifest and lived out all the time so it is a place of beauty, truth, salvation, justice, mercy and kindness. It runs parallel to the world in which we live now but will one day be fully revealed. One day perfection will come. I like thinking about it with reference to the well-loved children's book *The Lion, the Witch and the Wardrobe* by C.S Lewis. In that story, we read about four children who live in a war torn world. One day by accident, the youngest one Lucy, enters a wardrobe while playing hide and seek. She notices that the wardrobe has no back but that instead surprisingly it leads to a parallel world called Narnia where things are very different to reality as she knows it. This is a little like the way I picture the reign of God, it is an alternate world coexisting now within the world as we know and see it.

You can see glimpses of this alternate kingdom in the Old Testament through the story of Abraham. God promised him in Genesis 12:2 "I will make of you a great nation and I will bless you and make your name great, so that you will be a blessing. I will bless those who bless you and the one who curses you I will curse and in you all the families of the earth will be blessed". So here we see God's promise to extend his glory through all the earth. We also catch a glimpse of God's reign in some of the Psalms. Psalm 145 says, "All your works will give thanks to you O Lord, and all your faithful will bless you. They will speak of the glory of your kingdom and tell of your power, to make known to all people your mighty deeds and the glorious splendour of your kingdom. Your kingdom is an everlasting kingdom and your dominion endures throughout all generations."

It gets a little clearer when we reach the New Testament and Jesus erupts onto the scene saying in Mark 1:14 saying, "The time is fulfilled and the kingdom of God has come near, repent and believe in the good news." He says that the kingdom has "come near" rather than it has come, because it would more fully arrive at Jesus' death and resurrection. This ushered onto the earth God's reign in a more revealed way than ever before in the history of humanity. Humanity was able to know and experience the kingdom now. Jesus is the embodiment of the kingdom and entering the reign of God happens only through him. In the same way that the door to the wardrobe was the entry point to Narnia, an alternate world, Jesus is the door that opens wide the reign of God.

When Jesus walked the earth, many people thought Jesus the Messiah had come to establish a political kingdom. They wanted a kingdom of power like all the other kingdoms of the earth, a kingdom that would bring Israel fame and status like old times, a kingdom that would crush the Roman Empire and bring victory to the nation. They thought Jesus would be a king like all other earthly kings. Instead, Jesus revealed a different interpretation of the kingdom. It was not going to be a physical place. It would be more like a new reality, an alternative society, a new kind of quality of life where a relationship with God and other humans became right again. He taught about this new reality primarily using parables. Parables were pictures of the kingdom and only those with faith would be able to see and hear the truth. It is as though at the beginning of every parable Jesus was saying, "imagine if". Imagine a world where God runs to you like a desperate father (Luke 15:11ff), imagine a world where God gives because you ask (Luke 11: 13), imagine a world where you love your enemies (Matthew 5:43), imagine a world where you look out for the poor and they are raised to life (Luke 10:25ff). Moreover, Jesus displayed the kingdom by his powerful acts. His miracles and his healings all had a banner over them saying, "Imagine a world like this". The picture is of a world where death, sin and sickness is no more and instead life and *shalom* rule. This alternate reality and narrative has entered our world and has given us hope for today. The story will only end at the return of Jesus Christ when the reign of God will not merely be an alternate world coexisting with our broken world, but God's reign will be everything that we see and experience before us. Perfection will have arrived in the universe.

One of the best attempts to capture the essence of the reign of God that I know of is one of the songs from the musical *Les Miserables*. The song "Do You Hear the People Sing?" by composer Claude-Michel Schönberg conveys the hope, longing, desire and revolutionary spirit that are a part of the essence of the reign of God. Some of the images in this song come from Isaiah 2:1-4 that also depicts images of the beauty of the rule of God. Hear the longing for a better world in these words:

Do you hear the people sing
Lost in the valley of the night
It is the music of a people
Who are climbing to the light

For the wretched of the earth
There is a flame that never dies
Even the darkest night will end
And the sun will rise.

They will live again in freedom
In the garden of the Lord
They will walk behind the plough-share
They will put away the sword
The chain will be broken
And all men will have their reward!

Will you join in our crusade?
Who will be strong and stand with me?

Somewhere beyond the barricade
Is there a world you long to see?
Do you hear the people sing
Say, do you hear the distant drums?
It is the future that they bring
When tomorrow comes!

The evocative images in this song are glimpses of an alternative reality where God's presence permeates the earth. We can imagine pictures of the people of God walking towards the light; we can see portraits of justice, peace and compassion filling the earth, casting out the darkness. Is this the world we long to see? The story of the reign of God trumps all other stories and false narratives that we might be living. This is of course, the story of the gospel of good news and it is the story that we must tell and re-tell as we allow it to shape our lives that we might embody it in our local urban neighborhoods. Can you imagine a more inspiring, life giving and hope filled story for city dwellers than the one that I have just described?

The problem is however, that Christians have not often conveyed the gospel as this story of good news. Instead, we have presented a more truncated explanation of the gospel. We have turned the gospel into a set of abstract propositions that we assent to but it leaves us sometimes unaffected. Therefore, we believe the propositions with our minds but our behaviour remains unchanged. Think about what comes to your mind as you hear the word "gospel". Often we are taught and we rehearse four or so propositions that go something like this: God created the world good, we sinned and disobeyed God so deserved punishment, Jesus came into the world to offer us forgiveness of sins, if we accept Jesus into our lives as Lord and saviour we will not be punished but we will have eternal life with God. While these propositions are statements that many Christians will agree with, we can't say that this is the gospel fully fleshed out. The propositions convey one part of the gospel, an important part, but do not tell the whole story. Yet often when Christians hear the word "gospel" this is what they think. When I was growing up, this is the version of the gospel that was told to me. As soon as I repeated the "sinner's prayer", which was essentially a recitation of this four or five point gospel, I was a Christian and was supposed to accept these facts and then try to live my life as morally as possible.

Tim Foster in his book *The Suburban Captivity of the Church* helpfully sheds light on this truncated view of the gospel usually held by Christians. He differentiates between a punitive gospel and a telic gospel. A punitive gospel conveys that God created this world perfect but humans sinned so we are under God's condemnation. However, Jesus takes on our sin as we ask for forgiveness that means that we now have no condemnation in Christ. Our goal then here on earth is to live a holy life as we wait for the return of Jesus. On the other hand, a telic gospel centres on asking the question; how is God fulfilling his purposes for the world? In this version the story runs that God created the world, humans sinned and undermined God's world but Jesus took on our sin, he conquered evil and defeats death. The future is that there will be a new reality one day though it has begun already through the death and resurrection of Jesus. Presently, Christians are called to life in the light of this future, working with God on his mission in our world.[5] Foster says,

> One of the advantages of framing the gospel around God's purposes is that the present implications of the gospel are more obvious. We are not left waiting for heaven with no obvious implications for the present; we are beginning to transform our lives and the creation, in the power of the Spirit and in the light of our future hope. The new order means that there is a new way to life- a new way to be human, a new way to be community and a new way to relate to the world.[6]

So we can see that this way of viewing the gospel reads more like a story, puts more weight on Christians joining God's mission to create this new world and focuses more on God's purposes in a holistic way.

---

[5] Foster, *Suburban Captivity of the Church,* Loc 372.
[6] Ibid., Loc 403.

This more holistic view of the gospel is what I think we have been missing which stops us from communicating the gospel as story. This is a problem if we believe that stories shape our lives rather than primarily assent to abstract propositions. Instead, we have accepted a more abbreviated view of the gospel. Scot McKnight in his classic work *The King Jesus Gospel* says that this truncated view of the gospel reveals that Christians move in more of a "plan of salvation" culture rather than a broader evangelical one since we are not conveying the whole gospel *(evangelion)*. It means that Christians have skewed beliefs about God, who we are and what we are meant to be doing on earth. The book contains a brief quote from Craig, a student who was raised with this abridged version of the gospel. He says "At its heart, I have to say that I was raised by the gospel of fear...Growing up as a child I was given basic ideas; you're a sinner. We need you to be with Jesus. And he says us from hell...We always talked about how we are sinners and are drifting away from God and need to come to him before he 'has' to send us to hell."[7] This indeed is a very punitive way to view the gospel that focuses on salvation but doesn't mention the broader context and good news of the gospel. When I think about my understanding of the gospel as a new Christian, this is what seemed to be missing, that is, a broader story or context that helped place my faith in the present and ground me in the unfolding story of our world as well as my role in it.

The problem with living out this punitive version of the gospel is then that we compartmentalize our lives and we don't allow the gospel to affect us in the way

[7] Scot McKnight, "The King Jesus Gospel: The Original Good News Revisited," (Grand Rapids: Zondervan, 2011). Kindle Edition.loc 330.

that it must. We give assent to the propositions we have come to believe, but then we are unsure about how the gospel actually impacts our lives and satisfactorily answers meaning of life questions. In other words, there is a disconnect between what we believe and how we are living it out. The frightening truth could be that we are in reality living out the cultural narratives of our dominant culture that in the West carry traces of consumerism, individualism, racism, sexism and hedonism for example, but we remain unaffected by the story of the gospel. This is because we have placed "the gospel" in the form of a set of propositions, in a compartment of our lives rather than letting it affect every part of us. However, stories primarily shape our lives not belief in propositions. This is a huge problem for us if we are committed to working in urban places. A misunderstanding of the holistic gospel means we will misunderstand the reign of God since they are permanently intertwined. This alternate world called the rule of God conveys the good news of the gospel so if we simply understand the "plan of salvation" as being the whole gospel, we will be conveying to people in our local community a story that is less than "the Story". As a result people will not give up their lesser, dehumanizing and/or destructive cultural narratives and join with us in the Story that we are meant to be living out. In my faith journey before I started questioning this kind of compartmentalization, I saw no incompatibility between some of the self-destructive narratives I was living and my faith. The message that I received was that as long as I said and believed those four points of the gospel, I was a Christian and so in right standing with God.

As we understand, absorb and embody the story of the reign of God, ultimately what we want to do in our local communities is ask people to join with us as we live out this story with God. As we embody the rule of God in our inner city neighborhoods, we convey to people that the story is still ongoing and there is plenty of room for anyone to join with us. Anyone can enter through Jesus, live in this alternate reality and work with God on his mission as he brings restoration to our world that will gloriously climax at the return of Jesus Christ. I think that this brings us to the topic of evangelism for today. What does evangelism look like in an inner city context if we want to convey the story of the rule of God rather than presenting an abridged version of the gospel that is ultimately unhelpful? Scot McKnight shares,

> "How do you", I have been asked hundreds of times, "evangelize people into the kingdom?". But the problem I have with the question is that when people ask it, they use terms in unbiblical ways: when they use "evangelize" they mean "Plan of Salvation," and this gets us spinning in circles immediately. But kingdom and Plan of Salvation are like gospel and Plan of Salvation. They are two different sets of categories. The kingdom vision of Jesus isn't simply or even directly about the Plan of Salvation, though the kingdom vision entails or implies or involves the Plan of Salvation, and without the Plan of Salvation the kingdom doesn't work.[8]

I think that this is a helpful insight for us when we are thinking about presenting the gospel in the context of the inner city. If we simply present the "Plan of Salvation" as McKnight calls it, this can lead to a lack of authenticity as we formulate simplistic "gospel" presentations based on the four or five propositions of the salvation plan. This leads to compartmentalization rather than an embodiment of the Story of the reign of God as I mentioned previously.

---

[8] Ibid., Loc 496.

Instead I think that what we need to be doing is much more simple but harder in some ways. We simply understand the story of the kingdom of God, which is the gospel story, we embody this and we then invite others to join us. This stops compartmentalization in its tracks and instead we exist as urban missionaries living holy lives in the city grounded in our place, and welcoming others into God's story. We allow God's story to critique, purify any dehumanizing and destructive false narratives and we give our lives over to the story that matters and that leads to life. Considering what I have said about loneliness in the city and the need for true friendships, this is something that we need to think about with respect to "evangelism". A truncated view of the gospel can lead to seeing people as projects rather than human beings made in the image of God who are longing for God even though they may not know it. Elaine Heath in *Missional, Monastic, Mainline* critiques some forms of evangelism that sound good but have a hidden agenda. She says,

> Genuine friendships are relationships without an agenda. Friendship evangelism is never really about friendship when it has a church growth agenda. We have to give that up. It's just not the way of Jesus. What we do find in the Gospels is a way of Jesus who offers friendship to all sorts of people, some of whom decide to follow him.[9]

A holistic view of the gospel, which embodies the narrative of the story of the kingdom, sees people not as projects but rather as human beings who Jesus died for and invites to share with him in his abundant life. Genuine friendships are a better way of conveying this story rather than just presenting a salvation plan that is detached from the daily lives of the people around us.

---

[9] Elaine Heath, *Missional, Monastic, Mainline: A Guide to Starting Missional Micro-Communities in Historiclaly Mainline Traditions* (Eugene: Cascade, 2014), 26.

Christians are a foretaste of the alternate reality that Jesus called the kingdom of God. I love how Michael Goheen expresses this. He exclaims; "The words and actions, the very lives and communal life of Jesus's followers are to say: 'We are the preview of a new day, a new world. Because one day the world really will live as one. Won't you come and join us?' This is why the church has been chosen and given a taste of salvation. This is who we are."[10] As we embody the gospel and the story of the reign of God, we reveal to others in tangible form the majesty, humility and beauty of our creator. Our lives then ought to make people curious about the narrative we are living out. When they notice the scent of our Christ-like fragrance, they will want to join us and as we welcome these friends on the journey, we walk together, bringing light and being salt wherever we go until God's kingdom come. We tell people the Story is open, and we invite them to work together with us on God's mission to restore our world. Our eschatological hope is in the return of Christ at the renewal of all things but today we work knowing, as NT Wright says, "You are not restoring a great painting that is about to be thrown to the fire. You are not planting roses in a garden that is about to be dug up for a building site. You are strange as it might seem, almost as hard to believe as the resurrection itself- accomplishing something which will become in due course part of God's new world."[11] Our prayer is then "Lord your kingdom come in our neighborhoods. Your will be done in our urban communities as it is done in heaven."

---

[10] Michael Goheen, *A Light to the Nations: The Missional Church and the Biblical Story* (Grand Rapids: Baker Academic, 2011), 219.
[11] Wright, *Surprised by Hope*, page 3

Chapter Four:
Discernment

Jesus is deeply connected to the earth on which he walks. He observes the forces of nature, learns from them, teaches about them, and reveals that the God of Creation is the same God who sent him to give good news to the poor, sight to the blind, and freedom to the prisoners. He walks from village to village, sometimes alone and sometimes with others; as he walks, he meets the poor, the beggars, the blind, the sick, the mourners, and those who have lost hope. He listens attentively to those with whom he walks, and he speaks to them with the authority of a true companion on the road. He remains very close to the ground. ~ Henri Nouwen

I woke up that morning praying the same prayer that I pray every day "Lord give me your eyes and ears today as I move about in my neighborhoods. Show me your heart and help me to love those people around me who are my neighbours". I walked out of my apartment, onto the streets that I have become familiar with and strolled past the cafes and shops that I've come to know, all of which contribute to the story of my community. I had to get my haircut that day with a new hairdresser so I walked into the salon and sat in the chair as she began to work on my hair. We engaged in a bit of chitchat and the conversation was flowing nicely. I liked her. At one point, I was drawn to the crystal that she was wearing around her neck and I was curious. "I like your crystal; does it have some kind of spiritual significance for you?" I asked. She replied that she loved her crystal and took care of it to make sure that the energy within it grew. From that point, we started talking more deeply about spirituality and religion. She told me about her mother who cleansed houses spiritually if they had any kind of bad energies in them. She told me that while she believed in spiritual things, she thought that her mum went a bit "over the top" occasionally. She asked me what I did and I told her that I taught at a theological college. After explaining to her what that meant she asked me, "Do you ever find that your religion gets in the way of your spirituality?' I thought that was a great question and so we talked about this a little further as I kept answering her questions about Christian spirituality. I told her that I felt my religion grounded my spirituality. She found that comment interesting and it seemed to resonate with her because she felt that spirituality often can seem a little nebulous. She mentioned to me that she felt that some of her friends were occasionally a little too "kooky" when it came to spiritual matters. When I was about to walk out of the salon we smiled at each other and she thanked me for the conversation. I prayed under my breath "God thank you for giving me your heart for her. I pray that she might come to know your love more and more."

Another day I woke up and prayed a similar prayer as I stepped out into my neighbourhood. "God give me your eyes and ears. Help me to be a blessing today." I walked down to a café where I often get my breakfast and said hello to the waiter that usually serves me. We had developed a bit of a friendship and occasionally chatted but the conversations had always been superficial even though they were friendly. I asked him how he was that day and surprisingly he said, "It's just one of those days that I really don't want to be here." I asked why and he said something briefly about why he felt that way. I said that I hoped his day would get better. He thanked me. I walked out and prayed "God bless him today. May he experience your life and joy even though there is obviously something going on that is troubling him." Later on towards the end of the day, I walked past the café and saw him packing up the chairs and cleaning up after what looked like the leftovers of a very busy day. I asked him "Did your day get any better?" He swore and said that it had gotten worse. I said to him that I was sorry but that if it helped, I thought he was such a good waiter, that he had a gift in hospitality and I told him I always felt incredibly welcomed when I ate at the café because of him. A few tears welled up in his eyes and he said to me "That has just made my day, thank you."

I share these two stories not because I think that I have done anything particularly spectacular, quite the opposite, these are two stories I share to show how practicing everyday discernment in your local neighborhood can lead to "God moments" which contribute to God's mission in your community. Discernment is a characteristic of an urban spirituality. If we believe in and practice an incarnational Christianity, which grounds us in our neighborhoods, we will see our neighborhood as a sacred space filled with God's activity. If we believe that our neighbours bear the image of God and that "God is with us", then we will frequently be trying to connect with what God is doing in our local community. A "God is with us" spirituality will take seriously the presence of God in our lived environment, leading us to discern the Spirit working through the intricate ecosystem of the stories in our community. Living a missional life is simply about living a life of discernment. Discernment means that every day we ask two questions; "God what are you up to here?" Secondly, we ask, "How can I join with what you are doing here for your mission in this place?" Once we start living incarnationally, we will naturally be asking questions like "What is God doing today in my neighborhood?"

I think one way we discern the work of God in our local neighborhoods is by noticing the signs of beauty and life in the spaces where we live. We notice this not only through hearing the stories of people who live in our community, as I did with my two neighborhood friends, but also through paying attention to the built environment which also tells a story and therefore shapes a neighborhood.

In *Sidewalks in the Kingdom,* Jacobsen says that one marker of urban places is the beauty and quality of the built environment that can be found there. He says

> This can include buildings built by private companies that become important landmarks for a city, such as the Chrysler building in New York City. It can also include grand public buildings like city hall, the post office, or the country courthouse. Even projects like rose gardens or monuments become part of the local beauty. Non-profit organisations like churches, universities and theatre companies contribute to the beauty of a built environment as well. And homes, ranging from the grandiose to the quaint, especially in older neighbourhoods and in the downtown core, are often a source of community pride. Finally, the very act of planning the layout of the city itself- known as civic art- provides a source of beauty that can sometimes go undetected because it is so indirect.[1]

As I walk around my neighborhood, I can see that this is true. Careful attention is paid to civic art, planning and design of the neighborhood to maximise

---

[1] Jacobsen, *Sidewalks in the Kingdom,* Loc 1730.

beauty. The terrace houses are framed by lace-like ironwork that shows skill, the streets are lined with trees that attempt to bring life to what is often called the "concrete jungle" in the city and public artwork peppers the alleyways of my neighborhood. Of course, there is always the tension between the cultivation of beauty in a place, and urban development that often has more pragmatic goals in sight such as fitting in as many people into small spaces as possible. Usually, this does not make for beautiful places! Jacobsen does not deny this and neither does he deny that there are places of beauty in the suburbs and rural spaces. His point is that often, talented architects are drawn to the city and are able to exercise their abilities for planning and design there, in ways that maximise a city's beauty.

I noticed this as I took an "architectural tour" of my neighborhood with an official guide one day. Our group consisted of locals who wanted to get to know more of the beauty in their neighborhood. As I walked around my neighborhood, this architect tour guide told us about various buildings, and pointed to the design, I could sense that our group was feeling inspired as we learnt about the history of our community where we lived. But not only that, I also felt the Spirit had been at work in some of the craftsmanship of the buildings that we were exploring. Some of them were truly beautiful and in the same way that we can often sense the Spirit through a glorious piece of music, I sensed the presence of the Spirit who had been at work in some of the marvellous buildings we were looking at. Often people will have a sense of awe when they walk into old cathedrals and they experience something of the presence of God through the architecture designed to lift people's eyes and minds to ponder heavenly things. However, I often sense the Holy Spirit at work in the creation of public spaces, works of art and built environment in my neighborhood.

This makes for interesting discernment indeed, since it means that we are not only listening to the stories of people but also the stories of places, buildings, artworks and trying to discern the Spirit of God at work there. All of this contributes to helping us answer the question "Where is your mission here God?" This makes sense if we believe in a "God is with us" spirituality. God is not only active in the church; he is active in our world and even through our built environment. We "read" our environment and then discern God's presence as we hear the stories that come from our readings of those spaces.

Finding the beauty in urban places is a wonderful way of discerning the presence of God. If God is the author of beauty then we can ask not only of our natural environment, but also of our built environment, "God where can I see you in this?" and "What does this tell me about the place where I live and how can I join in your work?" Of course, we can also discern God when there is a lack of beauty. Firstly, we can see sometimes in urban spaces people who are experiencing pain, sorrow, and anything but beauty. The example of my waiter friend who was struggling with something that was putting a cloud over his day is a small example of that. We also see lack of beauty in our built environment. Councils can be corrupt, urban planning can be driven by pragmatism, lack of care, consumerism and greed rather than aesthetics and practices that are life giving. Often we see buildings and art in urban public spaces that do not contribute to building a positive city environment. Some of those buildings and public works of art contain stories nestled within them, which can be ugly and even horrific. I will share a few in the next pages. As we hear these ugly stories in the urban landscape this points to ways that we can contribute as those who embody a greater story, the story of the reign of God filled with hope, life and beauty. In the same way that beauty can point us to God, pain, ugliness and horror in our urban environment can also point us to the ways that God is at work if were are listening and willing to bless those places with God's healing and reconciliation. Again, this requires seeing discernment as a characteristic of urban spirituality. Often however, our Christian theology and practice has worked against the discernment of the presence of God in our lived environment.

Spirit-immersed Christianity

Some people have said that the Holy Spirit is the forgotten One in the Godhead. People seem to be able to relate to Jesus because he is human, the Father as provider but the Holy Spirit seems to be the one who we are not sure about. I often still hear people use the word 'it' to describe the Spirit rather than the more personal he or she. The Spirit is seen as a force that empowers people and places in order to do God's work and we are much more nervous praying to the Spirit or thinking about how to connect to his work for example.

However, we need to become a lot more comfortable in interacting with the Spirit if we are going to practice an urban spirituality once we start discerning

God's Spirit at work in the neighborhood. Instead of fearing, being confused by and overly cautious of the work of the Spirit, we should become Spirit-immersed Christians who are able to better discern his work in our neighborhoods. Practicing an urban spirituality means that we must become acquainted with discerning the Spirit at work. I think there are three elements relating to our theology that we need to keep in mind as we try to understand and become aware of the way that the Holy Spirit works in our contexts.

Firstly, we need to better grasp that the Holy Spirit is at work not only in our church but also in our world. We will usually agree that the Holy Spirit is the one who creates the church by his power and renews the church. Leaders will try and discern what the Spirit is saying in the church in order to implement plans and programmes in accord with God's will. That's the hope. However, it is also important to recognise that the Spirit is continually at work in the world. This counters a false dualism that says that the Spirit is in the sacred but not in the secular. If God is creator of the world and sustainer, then he is always at work in his world. There is actually, then, no such thing as the divide between sacred and secular because once we understand that God's presence is everywhere and always at work, everything can be seen as sacred. While it is certainly true that the church is a creation of the Spirit and is guided by, renewed and empowered by the Holy Spirit to be on God's mission, it is also the case that the Spirit is active in the world. It is the responsibility of the people of God to discern the activity of the Holy Spirit in the world since they are carriers of the Spirit, and connect with what God is doing in the broader world. Missiologist Craig Van Gelder admits this inadequate doctrine of creation as applied to the missional church has led to a lack of emphasis on what the Holy Spirit is doing in the world. He points to the ambivalence that the church has toward creation:

> Creation is viewed either as lacking God's presence or as the mere object of missionary work. In either case, it is understood largely as being without God-given worth and agency. Most striking is the lack of imagination of the Spirit's ongoing movement within creation, especially outside the church. A more robustly Trinitarian framework invites us into a deeper, more theological view of the world and God's continuing work of creation within it.[2]

A better Trinitarian framework and a more adequate theology of the Holy Spirit will help us to embrace a creation theology that highlights our context as a place where God is active as God invites us to join with his work. Sometimes Christian missionaries have a view that when they enter into a context they are "bringing God with them" while this is true in one sense because there is always the need to discern forces contrary to God in a context, it is also true that God has already been at work in that place before they arrive. Again, what is important is discerning that activity and joining with God's already active work.

There is a mutuality inherent in Christian spirituality that I think we often fail to understand. Instead of only seeing ourselves as the ones who bring the presence of God to a context, by discerning his presence already at work in the place, we engage in a kind of "mission in reverse" that exhibits a mutuality that is inherent in the Godhead. Mission in reverse, according to Anthony Gittins, means that the people of God are aware that God is not only at work in his church, but also at work in the world. This has two consequences. Firstly, it

---

[2] Dwight J. Zscheile and Craig Van Gelder, "*The Missional Church in Perpective: Mapping Trends and Shaping the Conversation,*" (Grand Rapids: Baker Academic, 2011). Kindle Edition.Loc 2404.

means that it reverses the usual view that God is only at work in his church. Secondly, it means that not only is the non-Christian impacted by the gospel through the Christian, but the Christian is also transformed by the Spirit of God at work through the non-Christian and his or her context.[3] Not only that, this also means that the Christian will be impacted by what he or she discerns as the Spirit of God moves in what might have traditionally been called a secular space. Gittins says that when mission in reverse is undertaken, it models true mutuality. He says:

> Jesus was constantly criticised for this palpable mutuality, for eating and consorting with "sinners", prostitutes, lepers, unclean people, outcasts, tax collectors and the rest. But he did not patronise them much less "use" them, they were his mission and ministry. They contributed to his transformation in mission as he encouraged and marvelled at theirs.[4]

This is an important concept to understand if we are going to practice discerning the Spirit in urban contexts. A clear understanding of how mutuality works is crucial for creating trust, authentic community and creative spaces to explore spirituality together.

A second idea to grasp about a theology of the Spirit, which will form us into Spirit –soaked Christians, is that the Holy Spirit conveys to us the immanence of God. We need to understand immanence as well as the omnipotence of God otherwise; we will have a view of God that is incorrect and unhelpful for learning how to discern the Spirit. One helpful contribution that theologian Stephen Bevans makes to this discussion is his focus on the 'transcending

---

[3] Anthony Gittins, *Bread for the Journey: The Mission of Transformation and Transformation of Mission* (Maryknoll: Orbis Books, 1993), 12.
[4] Ibid., 62.

immanence' of God. According to Bevans, this means that "God is genuinely involved in the world and its history – "not existence over and against but with and for, not domination but mutual love emerges as the highest value as the Spirit of God dwells within and around the world with all its fragility, chaos, tragedy fertility and beauty"[5] This points to the relational nature of the Spirit and that he works in the world bringing God's hope and life into it. The role of the people of God is to align with the imminent, edifying work of the Spirit and oppose anything that is contrary to the life-giving work of the Spirit.

As we understand that God is not only "out there", beyond us and all powerful but that God is also intimately close to us, as close as our very breath, and capable of mutuality and servanthood, we can begin to better understand how we might become Christians who practice discernment. We are discerning the presence of God who is so immanent that God delights to reveal himself to us often in surprising and unexpected ways if we have eyes to see this. I will elaborate this more in the pages to come but it is enough to say here that a theology of immanence is very important for our theology and our practice of an urban spirituality.

Thirdly, as we think about a theology of the Spirit that will shape us to be Christians who can discern the Spirit, we must understand that the Holy Spirit is not only our counsellor, teacher and comforter but she is also the one who sends us out on mission. It is the Spirit who sends and empowers people on the mission of God. As Christians are empowered by the Holy Spirit, they are then

---

[5] Stephen Bevans, "God inside Out: Towards a Missionary Theology of the Holy Spirit," *International Bulletin of Missionary Research* 22, no. 3 (1998): 104.

capable of working with God on his mission. We can see this in John 20:22 when Jesus sends his disciples on mission but breathes the Holy Spirit on them for their enabling. Whether this is a foretaste of what is to come at Pentecost or not is debatable, however it is clear that the disciples must receive the Spirit if they are to be successful. Moreover, this is also seen in Acts 1:8 when Jesus tells his disciples to wait until they have received "power when the Holy Spirit [comes]" before they are to go into the world to be his witnesses. It is clear that the Spirit is the one who propels us out onto mission. He can send us to "wild" and uncomfortable places also (Luke 4:1) yet this is something that we often fail to acknowledge.

Often, Christians prefer to highlight the role of the Spirit as our comforter, teacher and our counselor. The Spirit is interpreted as the one who is our friend, the one who does not leave us alone and also the one who teaches us God's ways. Of course, these are parts of the Spirit's characteristics that Jesus mentions in John 14:15ff. Yet we must also embrace the Spirit's characteristics that can lead us to strange places on God's mission, places we might not have suspected God would send us. If we keep in mind that the Spirit is not only our counselor and comforter but paradoxically she also sends us to uncomfortable places, we might be ready to start practicing discernment in urban places. Discernment therefore "can no longer be merely an in-house process when creation is understood to be infused with God's presence and activity. A much wider horizon of God's movement in and through so-called secular space, people and culture is needed. The church does not have exclusive possession of

God's presence and activity"[6] As we live this out in urban spaces, we will be able to practice an urban spirituality. There is much in our theology and culture however, which tries to impede us from doing this.

Distraction, Deism and Disenchantment

Like never before, we are a distracted humanity. Even if we argue that we are usually prone to juggling more than two things at once and flitting around from one thing to the next in search of a new adventure, today more than ever you could say that being distracted is a defining mark of what it means to be a 21st century human. We live in a world that offers us so many enticing shiny gadgets and thrilling experiences that we struggle to keep up. Not wanting to be left behind the advancement of modern technology, we purchase new products that promise to make our lives more efficient but paradoxically, turn us into busier people.

> Think about it. Even fifteen years ago you'd never have dreamed that in the near future you'd be able to: Make phone calls while riding in your car. Send mail electronically while riding in your car, while you are making phone calls. Own a machine that allows you to record your favourite shows so you can watch them when it's convenient for you- and you can even fast-forward through the commercials. Turn on your computer and be able to see on the screen the people you're talking to. There's no longer a need to travel for meetings.[7]

While these technological improvements have made us a more efficient people, we have also become a more distracted people. Distraction stops us from paying

---

[6] Craig Van Gelder, *Missional Church In Persepctive*, Loc 2425.
[7] Jay Pathak. *The Art of Neighboring,* Loc 457.

attention to the whispers of God's Spirit as God speaks to us about his mission right in front of our eyes.

Not too long ago writer and blogger Andrew Sullivan wrote an article in the New York Magazine that caused quite a stir. The article was called "I Used to Be Human" and it was controversial because Sullivan, a well-known blogger, was saying that he was giving up social media. After describing the negative effects of his addiction and obsession with constantly checking his phone, continually thinking about things that he needed to post in order to keep his followers, his lack of focus and inability to pay attention, he says,

> I tried reading books, but that skill now began to elude me. After a couple of pages, my fingers twitched for a keyboard. I tried meditation, but my mind bucked and bridled as I tried to still it. I got a steady workout routine, and it gave me the only relief I could measure for an hour or so a day. But over time in this pervasive virtual world, the online clamor grew louder and louder. Although I spent hours each day, alone and silent, attached to a laptop, it felt as if I were in a constant cacophonous crowd of words and images, sounds and ideas, emotions and tirades — a wind tunnel of deafening, deadening noise. So much of it was irresistible, as I fully understood. So much of the technology was irreversible, as I also knew. But I'd begun to fear that this new way of living was actually becoming a way of not-living.[8]

Sullivan is describing the unique way in which our social media saturated world causes us to be distracted to the point where it can be dehumanizing and rob us of truly living.

Distraction can also lead us to compartmentalising our lives. If we have so much new information, technology and ideas flying high speed at us constantly,

---

[8] http://nymag.com/selectall/2016/09/andrew-sullivan-technology-almost-killed-me.html

the only way we can cope is to form compartments in our lives that cater to the myriad things in life that we must juggle. Instead of an increase of focus and the ability to pay attention, this means we are continually switching from each compartment in order to cope with all of the stimulus around us. I think this can make us more impatient people who perhaps bypass the needs of others around us. We might become frustrated by the interruptions to our fast-paced lives that could in fact be quiet sounds of God's voice calling us to discern his presence.

We not only live in a distracted society but we are living in a society that has been identified as "disenchanted". Helland and Hjalmarson in *Missional Spirituality* state the question that Charles Taylor asked in his book *A Secular Age* as "What occurred between 1500 and 2000- the modern age of Western Society-when in 1500 it was impossible not to believe in God while in 2000 it became possible?"[9] The process and movement, according to Taylor is that of disenchantment. Disenchantment takes away the normalisation of spiritual things in everyday life. Whereas in the pre-modern era consideration, discussion and the integration of spirituality was a given, in modernity the rational, pragmatic and reason prevailed. Taylor would argue that this has shaped us into a people who have no room in our lives for things such as religion, spirituality and events such as miracles. This makes it harder to believe that the Spirit is at work around us and then to think about how to discern his ways in order to follow him on mission.

---

[9] Helland and Hjalmarson. *Missional Spirituality*, Loc 321.

Today, in my inner city community, people are still wary of spiritual things and my sense is that spirituality is not exactly normalized. However, people are becoming open to the possibilities that our world is spiritual rather than simply rational and physical in post-modern times. I have mentioned before that one time when having my haircut in my neighborhood, I was engaging with my hairdresser about spiritual matters as I asked about the crystal she was wearing around her neck. For her, the spiritual realm was normal as she told me about how her crystal gave her a sense of peace and confidence. Recently a well-known fortune-teller has moved into my neighborhood and set up shop on the main street. With a very big and eye-catching sign, he advertises his skills. His shop door is always open and I often see people in there to have their fortune told and their future predicted. Perhaps this is occurring more and more in our society today. People are longing to reconnect with spirituality, perhaps due to an overly long period of marginalization and an obsession in the West with rationalism.

Christians have bought into this culture of disenchantment. Often instead of embracing our spirituality and getting to know the invisible Spirit who guides us, we marginalize, rationalize and fear the role of the Spirit in our lives. Taylor says that when religion succumbed to disenchantment it was forced into the private realm. Taylor writes, "This was inconceivable in previous centuries...where religious values, practices, parishes, guilds and influences pervaded society. God, the Bible, churches, cathedrals, holidays, natural world, was a world "enchanted" with the spiritual world of God, spirits, demons and moral forces."[10] In a sense, the world of Christendom facilitated this enchantment. In the time of Christendom, bells rang to remind people in the parish to come to church, liturgies were all-of-life embracing and institutions in society made room for spiritual practices such as prayer and the Christian calendar. However, post-Christendom, modernity and Deism have all contributed to the secularisation of the practice of our faith today.

Deism emerged in the age of Enlightenment when scholars became disenchanted with the idea of miracles, supernatural revelation and concepts that were seen as too mystical such as the Trinity. With the backdrop of Isaac Newton's universal law of gravitation, he and others conveyed that God was like "a clock maker of the universe." God set everything in order and then stepped back, distant and removed, watching but not necessarily being involved with the day-to-day activities of our world. This is an overly simplified account of Deism, but my point is that while it is not new, I think many Christians today are deistic in their daily lives with respect to their relationship with God. Think about usual church meetings for example. Often we open up and close the meeting in prayer, however in between these two spiritual markers, we tend to run the meetings similarly to secular corporate board meetings. Moreover, my perception is that one of the reasons that people are beginning to engage with liturgy, such as Celtic prayers for example, more frequently today is in order to immerse and remind themselves of the presence of God in their daily lives. This is perhaps a response to a sense of lost confidence in the presence of God with us in an immediate and real way. Because of disenchantment infiltrating

---

[10] Taylor, *A Secular Age*, 26.

our faith and modernistic obsessions with reason and pragmatism, an engagement with the Spirit who intervenes in our day-to-day lives is something that we have quietly stopped practicing.

What occurs then is the practice of a hermeneutic of doubt. This way of seeing our world causes us to relate to God in a distant way without any attempt whatsoever to try to figure out whether he is interacting with us in more intimate ways than we might imagine. In other worlds, we become functional Deists. A functional Deist might believe in the theology of a personal God, but in practice, this Christian treats God as distant and struggles with the relevance of intercessory prayer for instance. However, Deism is not orthodox Christianity. Christianity believes in a very personal God who came as a human being and was intimately involved in the day-to-day life events of his time. After going to be with his Father, Jesus sent us the Holy Spirit that we might continue to experience the immanence of God in our lives. We miss out on the joy of a personal relationship with God if we give in to disenchantment, Deism and distraction.

We need this more open posture to the immediacy of the Spirit for our missionary purposes in the neighborhood. If our neighborhoods are places where God, by his Spirit is at work, then we must be comfortable with the view and practice of a personal God who will speak to us, guide us and delight to bring us into line with his mission. This is certainly not going to be a neat practice but rather it will be messy, there will be failures encountered and mistakes made. Moreover, we will need to embrace the mystery of God whereas we are normally more comfortable with the certainties of our faith. If we are going to practice an urban spirituality where discernment is necessary we must find ways to counter deism, disenchantment and distraction in order to pay closer attention to what the Spirit is doing in our local communities.

Discernment, Sacred Spaces and Re-Enchantment

We need to become more comfortable with the practice of discernment. I will say more about this in later chapters however; I think that many Christians today would like to be able to know how to discern God's presence but are not sure how to do this. As we practice discernment, we are able to live out an urban spirituality that joins with God on his mission.

If we are going to practice this discernment of the Spirit then we will need to live counter to our culture of distraction which stops us from hearing the whispers of the Spirit who is beckoning us to join with him as the Spirit builds the reign of God around and in us. This means paying attention to our surroundings. It means becoming aware of what is going on around us and realizing that God speaks as we listen, smell, touch and engage with what is going on around us. We will need to still and quieten ourselves in the midst of our busy lives, we will need to make space for hearing the messages that God wants to tell us, if we want to be his representatives and actors in living out his story in our neighborhoods. This does not have to be expressed in a way that means we retreat from our surroundings, although this is also a good practice that helps us to hear God. Practicing discernment can happen in our everyday lives as we go about our activities at work, in our social circles and also in our neighborhoods. I want to reiterate again, that we start paying attention and becoming aware of our surroundings, by asking two questions continually; what is God up to? How is God asking me to get involved in what he is doing? These are two simple questions that we keep in mind to practice discernment.

Practicing an urban spirituality will then mean moving our attention from the church to the neighborhood. Once we make the shift from asking, "What is God doing in the church?" to "What is God doing in my neighborhood?" this radically changes our perspective and makes us focus on the broader sphere of God's activity. Of course this does not mean we stop discerning God's presence in and words to the church, but as we make the neighborhood our focus, we join God on his mission in that very space. We become missionaries in our communities as opposed to only ministers of our church. We could say that the two distinct roles or gifts, pastor and missionary, merge in an urban spirituality.

For this shift to occur, we need to trust and believe that the Spirit is at work in our neighborhoods and that our local place is a context for the missionary activity of the Spirit. Alan Roxburgh explains that Christian practices must emerge from everyday contexts and so form us in that space. He says about this perspective, "It presumes the fitness of the ordinary as the primary location for discerning how God's agency shapes the life of the church. It claims that the everyday is the primary place where the God revealed in Jesus Christ is actively known and experienced. This is a basic shift in imagination."[11] This means practicing a theology that is holistic rather than dualistic. Instead of seeing only some spaces and places as sacred, it means seeing every space as a potential context for the presence and activity of God. As Roxburgh says, it means becoming comfortable with a spirituality of the ordinary, which sees that this context is a fit place for the purposes of God.

This spirituality of the ordinary is of course an aspect of urban spirituality, and the notion of sacred space is very relevant here. As you walk around the urban neighborhood where you live, do you see it as a sacred space? Or perhaps more specifically, can you discern any sacred spaces in your neighborhood? Once we make the shift from discerning God's presence primarily in the church to the neighborhood, we will begin to see certain places that hold special meaning and carry significance in our local community. You could say that these places are seen as sacred to the locals in a particular neighborhood.

One example of sacred space in my inner-city community is a story that contains both horror and redemption. Several years ago, a woman was brutally gang raped late at night in a laneway in my neighborhood. Her pleas and cries for help went unheard on that terrible night. When this atrocious act came to light and the local community discovered what had happened, they were outraged. The community wanted to do something to redeem the space that had become known as a place of horror. They also wanted to take a stand against violence towards women. They wanted to somehow convey that this

---

[11] Alan Roxburgh, "Practices of Christian Life- Forming and Performing a Culture," *Journal of Missional Practice* Autumn, (2012).

sort of thing was unacceptable in our community. So community groups were consulted and an artist was commissioned to create an artwork at the very scene of the crime that would convey the story of what happened. The artist constructed a beautiful pink lamp that remains lit at night on that laneway. On the walls of the building there in red these words are written,

This is a lane with a name and a lamp in memory of the woman who survived being beaten and raped here. She happened to be lesbian. When the sun sets this lamp keeps vigil along with you who read this in silent meditation.

The artwork was set there to be a tribute to all women who have experienced violence and as a sign of hope and courage for the gay community who are strongly represented in my neighborhood.

My sense when I visit this laneway which is just off the street where I live, is that more than being a tribute to women, it has become a sacred space in my community. I have seen women and men go there occasionally and light candles, some of them pray or stand in "silent meditation" as the words on the wall say, in order to pay respect to the victim. It is a space for meditation, remembering and reflecting on the darkness and hope that lies in humanity. I often marvel at the bold move that our local council made to establish such a confronting, disturbing and redemptive piece of street art in my neighborhood. I'm glad for it because my neighborhood is unafraid to highlight beauty but also to boldly remind us of the hatred we are capable of which needs to be challenged and rejected in our community.

In Phillip Sheldrake's book *The Spiritual City: Theology, Spirituality and the Urban*, he mentions a few ways that solidarity among strangers can be built. This he argues, is most of all important in cities which have a reputation for and a habit of representing loneliness, isolation, crime and disparity of wealth. One concept for building solidarity in the city is the notion of 're-enchantment'. He defines it like this: "Re-enchantment seeks to make public space more than a context for human socialization created purely by consumerism or tourism. Rather, we should work imaginatively and experimentally with public space to make it the medium for a transformation of imagination and behavior through protest gatherings (non-legislative politics), art, education and entertainment."[12]

If disenchantment is about extracting anything remotely spiritual from everyday life and places, re-enchantment brings a sense of the sacred back into our daily lives. I think that's what I discern in this story from my local community. A horrendous act was perpetrated by violent men, but instead of turning its back, a community came together to build a memorial which would function as a sacred space — a reminder of the deep worth and respect we must have for all human beings. The hope, presumably, was that all who pass by would be encouraged to practice peace, hospitality and mutual honor rather than the violence illustrated in the crime. This is not simply a gruesome reminder of an atrocious act — the memorial carries a vision for transformation. The community used their collective imagination in order to

---

[12] Sheldrake, *The Spiritual City*, Loc 375.

change neighborhood behavior, and in that process, a sacred space was created on the streets of my neighborhood.

What I see in this story is an example of re-enchantment. The difference in this story and others today however, is that sacred space is not being experienced primarily in the cathedrals, churches and other normally "holy" places. Instead, it's on the streets, lanes, alleyways, cafes, pubs and bars of the city. Christendom gave us cathedrals as sacred spaces in contrast to the profane, but in a society that is post-Christendom, we more clearly see that the sacred spills out onto the streets, mixing with the horror and beauty of humanity. The holy mixes with the profane, heaven touches dirt, and peace mingles with turbulence. In essence, this is the 'enchanting' truth of the incarnation. The most stirring realization we can have is that the Holy merged with fleshly, sinful humanity and co-existed.

Where are the sacred spaces in your neighborhood? Sheldrake says that sacred spaces such as parks, art museums count in this category. He states, "Whatever form it takes, a sacred space is likely to contain powerful symbols of a community's creativity, aspirations, and quest for self—transcendence. It will be a kind of sanctuary from the pace of city life- a space for silence, for thinking, even for a kind of healing."[13] Or the sacred spaces could function like shrines, as in my story of horror and redemption in my neighborhood. This means having a sacramental view of place. John Inge says that having a sacramental view of place is best described as having "sacramental encounters" in particular

---

[13] Ibid., Loc, 3161.

places[14]. He attributes this to Christians in churches but I think that we can apply this to our neighborhoods if we truly believe that God is at work there and that our local context is a sacred place of God's missionary activity. Interestingly he also says that these spaces function as shrines, which can have an eschatological function.[15] Sacred spaces can point to a hope deep within humanity, of a better world. The Spirit of Jesus is at work in our local neighborhoods to fulfil that hope and it is up to us to see it, point that out to others and then engage with God's redemptive activity there.

---

[14] John Inge, *A Christian Theology of Place* (Hampshire: Ashgate, 2003), 89.
[15] Ibid., 114.

Chapter Five:
The Other

It may not be too much to claim that the future of our world will depend on how we deal with identity and difference ~ Miroslav Volf

Scripture does not teach that the stranger is not strange to us or that the differences among us are somehow insignificant. But however different, "the other" represents neither metaphysical danger nor darkness. When one's life is "hidden in Christ" the existence of the other neither threatens or diminishes ~ James Davison Hunter

When I was thinking about moving into my inner-city neighborhood, my real estate agent told me about the attractions, advantages and local stories of the area. "Of course, you also have a shopping center just a five minute walk away. The famous Murder Mall as the locals call it", he said with a smile and then a chuckle. Murder Mall? That didn't sound very appealing I thought, even though his manner seemed very relaxed as he shared this. I thought it was a bit odd that a real estate agent was telling me something that sounded distasteful about my potential new neighborhood, though maybe he wanted to convey to me that my neighborhood was "colourful". So I asked him about "Murder Mall" and he told me the story.

My local shopping centre is of course where all the locals do their daily grocery shopping. The centre is small; some would say it's a little run down and not up to the standards of the rapidly gentrifying community in which I live. But I like the shopping centre because it is a space where all members of the community mix together to do a very human, ordinary and mundane thing like shop for basic items. I like it because it is unpolished, down-to-earth and authentic. Many people in my inner-city community are on the margins of society. Many are homeless, many more struggle with mental illness, which means that they are misunderstood frequently, feared, and ostracised by others. All of them struggle with issues around lack of social connection, poverty and are sometimes, because of their vulnerability, victims of violence.

As these people are part of my community, they of course do their shopping in my local community center; they also congregate there sometimes to rest, eat, drink or sleep. Sometimes they are "invisible" in the sense that no one pays much attention to them, other times they might be a little more rowdy, disoriented and loud so they attract a lot of attention. The story of "Murder Mall" is that one person started taking photographs on a smartphone of some of these people around the shopping center. The photos taken were of those who were homeless, those struggling in life for the reasons I have mentioned in positions that were, to say the least, unflattering. The photos of these dishevelled people were taken to make fun of, laugh at, and mock the people who are part of this community. An Instagram account was set up and others joined in, taking photos of those already marginalised members of my neighborhood and posting them on social media. It became quite popular to take more and more embarrassing photos of people in order to get a laugh and increasing "shares" and "likes" on social media.

However, many people in my community, especially the charities that are based there, became irate about what was happening. They were outraged that vulnerable people were being mocked and abused in this way. These charities especially exist to take care of and help the vulnerable in my community so I can imagine how appalled they were after gradually discovering what had been happening. So after some time, the Instagram account was shut down due to pressure from many in my community who were lamenting the further marginalisation of people who were already struggling with fitting into society.

When I heard this story and then did a little research around it, I was along with many others, appalled. I became aware that there are people in my community who think it is funny to mock marginalised and vulnerable people. However, equally, I also became aware of others in my community who like me, think that this dehumanization of people is not to be tolerated. It revealed a tension in my community between those who have very little power, status and material goods, those who are disadvantaged, and those who are the well-off. Since then, I have continued to notice a tension that usually lies beneath most interactions, public meetings and decisions made. However, it sometimes surfaces and the tension is exposed as a real issue that needs more community attention. In one meeting, I was participating in, open to all members of my neighborhood, we had gathered to share our stories about our community. As we each shared our experiences of the area, the issue of gentrification came up. One woman in the group bemoaned the fact that the area was getting more gentrified and this was making it appear too polished and unfriendly to the less well off. "*Getting* gentrified!" another woman scoffed. "This area is already completely gentrified. That's why I moved out." I remember sensing a lot of anger in her voice.

Urban spaces are known for their diversity. I have already mentioned the fact that the city is a place that gravitates towards heterogeneity rather than homogeneity. In my community, there are many sub-cultures that need to dwell in peaceful coexistence with one another. Once I was doing a project in my community for our neighborhood center, which required me to talk with strangers on the street and ask them their thoughts about their quality of life. In the space of two hours, I spoke with a group of South American students studying in my city, a local real estate agent who thanked me for what I was doing in my community, a family from the suburbs who just love my neighborhood and were there to celebrate the parent's wedding anniversary, a baby boomer who was looking to buy in the area because she felt it had more life than where she lives now, a woman who had a recent death in family and was re-thinking what the purpose of life is, a transgender woman in recovery from drug addiction, two students from Singapore visiting my city, a local who has lived in the area for 20 years and had very strong views about the change happening in the community, and a young guy who was from another state and had come to Sydney to "pick up some money from a friend" so that he could start his own show and get famous. This was a very startling and confronting snapshot of the different sub-cultures that exists simultaneously in my little inner city village. In this sense the city is a place where "the other" exists and in close proximity. By "the other", I mean that difference exists in a more concentrated sense in the urban space. This of course has potential to be very rewarding because you are able to meet interesting people and learn from them but also very challenging because it can cause tensions, misunderstanding and fear.

Eric Jacobsen says that another mark of urban spaces is it is a place where we encounter strangers. He says, "In a city you come to expect that many people you will see throughout your day are going to be strangers. There is not, therefore, a stigma attached to being a stranger. Cities are among the few places where strangers are accepted, and consequently, people who have no significant network of people come to cities because they can."[1] I would extend this notion of a stranger that Jacobsen uses and apply it not only literally, as in those who move in and out of the city, but also to mean those who we find strange and *other* to us even though we live together in the same neighborhoods. One critique I would make of Jacobsen's mark of urbanity here is that the term "strangers" could imply that certain people are not a crucial part of the community in which they actually live. Some people might seem "strange" or transient to those of us who are perhaps more privileged, however, these people also make their home in our neighborhoods. I would prefer to see it as all of us seeing one another as somewhat strange to each other. The city is a context where different subcultures exist together and so we must navigate what peaceful coexistence looks like. Within this, we must especially advocate for the poor, the vulnerable and the stranger, as Jesus would direct us. Jacobsen does address this to some extent, when he mentions that the stranger should not be

---

[1] Jacobsen, *Sidewalks in the Kingdom*, Loc 2432.

seen as the problem but rather as one aspect of a problematic system, which can for instance create and perpetuate poverty[2].

The stranger can mean the tourist or traveller who passes in and out of our neighborhood. The city is a place that attracts more visitors and so it is not uncommon for locals to be used to seeing visitors to their neighborhoods. The stranger can also mean the poor, homeless and marginalized who pass through or live in our neighborhoods. The stranger can also mean those who have recently moved in, who are more privileged and who will need to come to terms with the different sub-cultures and diversity of people in the new neighborhood they now inhabit. As my story about Murder Mall shows, tensions exist not only because of the struggles of the marginalised but also because of the negotiations of expectations and needs that must be managed between the various groups of people who live in our community.

Jacobsen says that this puts Christians in a unique position if they choose to live in urban spaces. As we live in close proximity and move about in the public spaces, which make up part of our urban environment, we will encounter the other. Jacobsen notes, "Conversely, by choosing to live or work in cities, where strangers actually are to be found, we put ourselves in a position to be obedient to Christ's command concerning the stranger."[3] For those who live in the city I think Mother Theresa's words here are apt and heart-warming.

> Stay where you are. Find your own Calcutta. Find the sick, the suffering and the lonely right there where you are — in your own homes and in your own families, in your workplaces and in your schools. You can find

---

2 Ibid., Loc 2480.
3 Ibid., Loc 2458.

Calcutta all over the world, if you have the eyes to see. Everywhere, wherever you go, you find people who are unwanted, unloved, uncared for, just rejected by society — completely forgotten, completely left alone.[4]

There are people in our neighborhoods who we can show the love of Christ to and this will bring healing to our community. Jacobsen also says, "There are strategies that we can employ, wherever we live, that might begin to heal a culture that has forgotten how to welcome the stranger."[5] I think that this is where spirituality in an urban context can thrive and contribute to the city in which we live.

As we move into or live in the city and recognise the presence of the other in the urban contexts where we live, it is an opportunity to practice a spirituality that will bring healing and life to the contexts where we live. The presence and proximity of people who are different can be a context for Christians to practice an urban spirituality that relates to this environment but also brings blessing to the context in order to join with God's mission in the neighborhood. What kind of a spirituality would be appropriate for this sort of setting? We have looked at focusing on community, incarnation and discernment in the city context and now we look at the final mark of an urban spirituality- that of *kenosis*.

---

[4] William Murdock, *Find Your Own Calcutta: Living a Life of Service and Meaning in a Selfish World* (BloomingtonL WestBow Press, 2017), page 2.
[5] Jacobsen, Loc 2475

Kenotic Christianity

The word *kenosis* is found in Philippians 2:7 referring to how Jesus "emptied himself" and willingly chose to become a servant by limiting his divine glory and becoming human. Jesus engaged in "self-emptying" in order to become human so that he would be able to serve humanity through dying on a cross for the glorification of God. We can see four aspects of this self-emptying or *kenosis* in Philippians 2:6-8.[6] Firstly, the Son voluntarily chose to humble himself and engage in *kenosis*. That "he emptied himself" (v. 7) implies a voluntary act that was chosen by Christ rather than something that was forced upon him. Secondly, the *kenosis* implies a self-giving, an emptying of self-focused desires and instead taking on the posture of a servant. Thirdly, the passage refers not to one act of *kenosis* on the cross but of three actions. In verse 3, it can be seen that the Son refused to take advantage of his divinity; in verse 7, the Son takes on the nature of a human being, and in verse 8 he died on a cross. These are three separate steps in which the Son engaged for the process of *kenosis* to be complete. Fourthly, Jesus' kenotic act was based on obedience to the Father and we can see this in verse 8 when he "became obedient to the point of death". This is helpful because we often mostly focus on the act of crucifixion as Jesus' expression of *kenosis,* however Jesus gave himself up, became a servant in various ways. His incarnation, life, service to others and death were all acts of *kenosis* displaying his cruciform way of life.

Kenosis then is not something that God merely does but rather it is something that he is. God is a God who is cruciform or kenotic. *Kenosis* flows from the

---

[6] Michael Gorman, *Cruciformity: Paul's Narrative Spirituality of the Cross* (Grand Rapids: Eerdmans, 2001), 91.

divine triune identity is which God is an interpersonal communion of love. Ross Hastings who points to the eternal wounds of Christ from the crucifixion poetically sums this up.

> When the Lamb is worshipped in heaven, it is perpetually depicted as freshly slain (Rev 5:6). The wounds of Christ, it would seem, will be a source of wondering adoration throughout eternity, in the new creation, and, no wonder, for they are the source of reconciliation and renewal of that creation. That at the heart of the reconciliation of all things is the Son of God slain is evidence enough that this is at the heart of God's intentions for the universe he created.[7]

If the wounds of Christ are everlasting and a source of adoration then it could be said that the nature of God is kenotic.

God's very nature is kenotic; however, it is also the case that the people of God must reflect this nature and the church must develop into a cruciform community. Only in this way will the people of God live for the sake of the world as missionaries to their local context. David Bosch says, "The scars of the risen Lord do not only prove Jesus' identity, however, they also constitute a model to be emulated by those he commissions "As the Father has sent me so I send you".[8] This notion of modelling the *kenosis* of Jesus is also seen in Philippians 2 where Paul writes of Christ's *kenosis* but prefaces it by saying, "Let the same mind be in you that was in Christ Jesus" (v5). In the Gospel of Luke, Jesus said that in order for a person to find their life they would need to lose it by taking up the cross and engaging in self-denial (9:23-24). This is the process of *kenosis* to which Philippians 2 refers, however here Jesus is saying

---

[7] Ross Hastings, "*Missional God, Missional Church*," (Downer's Grove: Intervarsity Press, 2012). Kindle Edition. Loc 3021.
[8] David Bosch, *Transforming Mission: Paradigm Shifts in Theology of Mission* (Maryknoll: Orbis Books, 1991), 514.

that he expects the same of his followers. Ron Clarke points out that as Luke was writing for the context of the early church, this would have acted as a reminder to them to keep focused on the selfless life of Jesus. This would encourage the early church as they were persecuted for their beliefs. He says, "Luke reminded (the early church) that carrying the cross to Jerusalem meant fully embracing Jesus' ministry... by setting his face to the city he proved to his disciples, as well as the readers that discipleship calls for courage, vision and conviction."[9] God wants his people to be kenotic too.

Two things are important to keep in mind when we talk about a kenotic Christianity. Firstly, *kenosis* is something that we practice day in day out. It is not something that we do occasionally. This means that we must live cruciform lives, or lives that are shaped by the cross. Michael Gorman says, "Cruciformity is an ongoing pattern of living in Christ and of dying with him that produces a Christ-like (cruciform) person. Cruciform existence is what being Christ's servant, indwelling him and being indwelt by him, living with and for and "according to" him, is all about, for both individuals and communities."[10] In this sense, we can speak of a continual *kenosis* occurring in the Christian's life. Since the Christian has been co-crucified with Jesus (Galatians 2:19, Romans 6:6), the life of a Christian is about self-emptying and posturing oneself as a servant of God and others. This counters the practice of dualism that sometimes occurs in the life of a Christian whereby we might perform spiritual

---

[9] Ron Clarke, "*Jesus Unleashed*," (Eugene: Cascade, 2013). Kindle Edition. Loc 4163.
[10] Gorman, *Cruciformity: Paul's Narrative Spirituality of the Cross*, 48-49.

acts but they do not produce inner transformation of the heart. A life of cruciformity makes this impossible.

> We often prefer both to compartmentalise and to routinize our lives, not only in terms of inconsequential habits but also in terms of our spirituality. It is not uncommon for people, though perhaps not consciously or deliberately, to separate their 'spiritual' or religious beliefs and practices from their behaviour... Cruciformity does not permit any of this... Each Christian can therefore ask 'In what part of my life story is the story of the cross not being told?[11]

Cruciform is something we are and this then leads to what we do.

I remember once a member in my church who was a merchant banker, telling me that he felt it was impossible to live the kind of life that Jesus advocated in his sermon on the mount for instance. He told me that at church he was able to grasp the beauty and significance of love of enemies and self-surrender for the sake of others. However, his workplace culture and practices made it impossible for him to live this ideal out. As a result, he told me he had decided to live one way when at church, but then submit to the practices of his cutthroat workplace context when he was there. This poor person was simply using the tactic of compartmentalization in order to be able to survive as a banker. However, cruciformity does not allow us to live in this ultimately dualistic and disparate manner.

Secondly, living a cruciform life means a redefining of the notion of power. In Philippians 2:6-7, it is clear that God is a God who, rather than exerting his power, manifests power through weakness. Cruciformity redefines power so that status, privilege and rights become questionable uses of power and notions

---

[11] Ibid., 382.

such as weakness, humility and service are affirmed instead. Gorman points to three consequences of the experience of power as weakness in daily life.[12] He states firstly that the experience of power is no longer limited to the powerful. Normally, the view of power is that only powerful people can exert it. However, with power redefined through the cruciform God, any person can exert power since weakness is a trait of this redefined form of the concept. Secondly, he says that "normal" i.e. worldly experiences of power prove to be something else, and thirdly, that experiences of weakness can in fact be experiences of God's power. This latter point is crucial since it is the normative way that Christians must be thinking about and experiencing power. Power is characterized by weakness in a cruciform life. This subversive way of viewing power from a Christ perspective to be sure, is counter the culture and can be misinterpreted to function as a way to control or dominate. However, the point is that *kenosis* turns worldly concepts of power upside down and it is this expression of power that Christians must practice.

Kenotic Christianity as you can imagine, is helpful for us in terms of how we view and engage with the other in the expression of our urban spirituality. As we think about living cruciform lives and practicing a reign of God form of power, this will impact how we engage with those around us in our inner-city neighborhoods who are different to us. David Augsburger brings out this aspect of self-sacrifice in *Dissident Discipleship*. He states, "We are co-buried, co-crucified, we have co-died and now we co-live, co-inherit and co-suffer as we

---

[12] Ibid., 397.

are co-glorified and co-formed into the son of God's image to become sisters and brothers in Christ."[13] As a result:

> Following Jesus as his disciple does not call for obliterating our mimetic desires , on the contrary it demands that they be redirected, reoriented and refashioned away from selfish, acquisitive and violent forms of mimesis to patterns of imitation that are forgiving, other regarding, peaceable , loving and marked by humble service.[14]

I like the way that Segundo Galilea applies this Christian concept of crucifomity, self-surrender and living lives of service to others, to a special focus on the poor, weak and marginalised in our community. He says,

> Mission is to leave one's own geographic or cultural Christian world in order to enter the world of even the poorest and the most unchristian. The non-believer, the fallen away Christian, the poor and the oppressed are always the subject of missionary love, and the more mission leaves its own world in search of them, the more it is radicalised and the closer it approaches the model and desire of Christ.[15]

As we die to ourselves daily as Christ commanded us (Luke 9:23) and we live lives which are cruciform, we become "radicalized" as we imitate Christ in his loving service to others especially the poor. Living lives of surrender, peace and service to others is an expression of urban spirituality as we engage with the other in the city. However, there are factors in our culture that try to stop us from living in this way.

Fear, the Idolatry of Safety and Narcissism

Living out a kenotic Christianity in the inner city has an element of risk about it. If we are open to mixing with and not only that but also welcoming those

---

[13] David Augsburger, *Dissident Discipleship* (Grand Rapids: Brazos Press, 2006), 38.
[14] Ibid., 40.
[15] Segundo Galilea, *The Way of Living Faith: A Spirituality of Liberation* (New York: Harper and Row, 1988), 157.

who are different to us, this is going to force us out of our comfort zones and into places that we might usually run away from. I am frequently challenged by this in my day-to-day life. I will gravitate towards people who are like me and who have my values however; it takes more effort to connect with those who do not share my beliefs and practices. For instance, I can say that my community needs to connect with each other more and that the different sub-cultures must blend better. However, when I am faced with a person sitting next to me at the local bus stop who smells, looks dishevelled, swears at me and acts unkindly, I am forced to put into practice showing kindness in order to build connections in my community. This requires me stepping out of my place of comfort, taking a risk and showing love even though it may not be rewarded or even recognised. It also means building connectivity and relationship in the midst of perhaps feeling somewhat fearful. This is something that our culture discourages. We live in a culture that leans towards idolising safety and comfort in order to minimise risk, protect and control our environment. This can stop us from practicing *kenosis* because instead of forgetting ourselves and thinking of others we move towards self-protection, which stops us from engaging with those who are different to us.

In an essay titled "Fear" in her book *The Givenness of Things*, Marilynne Robinson writes, "There are always real dangers in the world, sufficient to their day. Fearfulness obscures the distinction between real threat on one hand and on the other the terrors that beset those who see threat everywhere".[16] Today we live in an atmosphere of gratuitous fear. It has become such a part of our

---

[16] Marilynne Robinson, *The Givenness of Things* (London: Virago, 2015), 126.

environment that we find it hard to identify when it rises up in our hearts and stomachs. Fear of those who are different to us thrives and it inhibits hospitality, true friendship and deep trust. Deb Hirsch explains in the book *Untamed* how fear builds walls rather than connections between people. She says that our normative perspective is that

> This is "our" space, and those we may "invite" into that space are carefully chosen based on whether they will upset the delicate status quo, inconvenience us, or pose a threat to our perceived safety. In other words, visitors, especially strange ones, stress us out. And while this is in some sense culturally understandable, the negative result in terms of our spirituality is that the family has effectively become a pernicious idol.... Culture has once again trumped our social responsibility. In such a situation, missional hospitality is seen as a threat, not as an opportunity to extend the kingdom; so an idol is born. It's not hard to see how this is absolutely disastrous from a missional perspective. Our families and our homes should be places where people can experience a foretaste of heaven, where the church is rightly viewed as a community of the redeemed from all walks of life. Instead, our fears restrict us from letting go of the control and safety we have spent years cultivating.[17]

This is devastating for an urban spirituality that has a kenotic element that seeks to bring peace, healing, welcome and unity among the different sub-cultures that exist in the city neighborhood.

I was struck again as I read the book of Acts recently by the provocative and life-changing concept of resurrection. Because we know that this world is not all there is, because we know that we will rise again, because our hope is not only in the now but also in the not yet, we have nothing to lose. We know that the early Christians put this into practice. In the third century when a devastating plague swept across the ancient world, the Christians were the ones who went

---

[17] Deb Hirsch Alan Hirsch, "Untamed: Reactivating a Missional Form of Discipleship," (Gand Rapids: Baker Books, 2010). Loc 2363.

out onto the streets to care for the sick and diseased. They took the risk of being infected by the disease themselves. Some who were not Christians left their infected family members to die rather than risk being themselves infected. We still see examples in the world today where many Christians take the risk to live in parts of the world that are places besieged with pain, death and stigma.

Urban Neighbors of Hope (UNOH) is an organisation that has a practice of sending missionaries into parts of cities in the world that are devastated and marginalized by the government and local communities. A friend of mine who works for UNOH and his family moved into one such place in Sydney in order to serve the people there and bring to light the potential and beauty that exists in that neighborhood.[18] Surely, resurrection is foremost in the thoughts of people like this. Death cannot ultimately harm them since they are looking forward to the New Jerusalem in a restored universe. The cross is not enough; instead, living out the resurrection is what will change our world. Where is this kind of abandon and embodied hope in the community of God's people today?

This existence of fear, self-protectionism and idolatry of safety is unhelpful yet existent in the context of cities that are becoming more gentrified. Many of those that we might call "strangers" have lived in the urban context long before those who are more socioeconomically advantaged began to move in. Jacobsen helpfully explains the process of gentrification

> Many of our cities are neglected and in great disrepair. However, they continue to be home for many members of our society and a source of low cost housing for the people at the bottom of our socio economic

---

[18] http://www.smh.com.au/lifestyle/life/house-of-hope-20120118-1q62h.html

ladder. When people in a higher socioeconomic class "rediscover" a city, they move in and begin to revitalise the region, thus creating more of a twenty-four-hour city. This leads to even more interest in moving to the region, and real estate prices begin to escalate. This first hits the renters, who are forces out of the area by rising rents. And, in times, it can hit the homeowners, as they see their property taxes go through the roof. What therefore can happen is that an area in the city is revitalised, but all of its original residents have to move out.[19]

Gentrification can help to make a city safer, diverse and residential however; it can bring to the surface fear, which promotes mistrust, and build a fortress mentality. This stops people from interacting with each other and benefitting from the diversity that exists in the community.

A great inhibitor to practicing kenosis is of course narcissism and our culture thrives on this narrative. Cloaked as healthy ambition, self-esteem or even being vulnerable in a public forum, narcissistic tendencies abound in Western culture. Obviously, ambition, self-esteem and vulnerability are all good things but with an undercurrent of individualism and self-promotion in our culture, these good values become distorted and bloated with self-importance. There is a wonderfully visual description of our human tendency towards selfishness given to us by St Augustine who called our fallen condition an "incurvature of the soul".[20] As you can probably picture, this is a tendency towards turning inwards rather than turning outwards to God, each other and our world.

There is a slightly humorous but sad old tale in the Rabbinic tradition that tells about a prince who lived in a faraway land a long time ago who longed for true

---

[19] Jacobsen, *Sidewalks in the Kingdom,* Loc 2622.
[20] Matt Jenson, *The Gravity of Sin: Augustine, Luther and Barth on 'Homo Incurvatus in Se'* (London: T&T Clark, 2007), 59.

community where each person showed loyalty and sacrificial service towards each other. So he called a meeting of his leadership to discuss this. As a part of the first gathering of this meeting, which would start discussions about how to turn this land into a true community, he called each leader to bring their best wine produced from their ancestral vines. These wines would be poured into a communal vat and blended as a representation of true community. One of the winegrowers wondered how he would do this, as it would compromise his wine. The unique grapes that he used would be spoiled; no one would be able to taste the uniqueness of his wine taken from his special vineyard. So the night before the great meeting, he poured water into a wine bottle and took it to the meeting thinking that no one would notice. The next day the meeting started and the prince asked all to pour their wines into the one giant vat. Excitedly the prince then asked the leaders to take from the vat and drink as a symbol of community. They did so and discovered they were all drinking water. None of the leaders had wanted to compromise their wine. No one was willing to let go of their own self in order to create true community. Truly surrendering to each other feels as if we are losing our sense of self to some extent, and in our narcissistic society where individualism reigns, this is anathema. However, if our identity is grounded in Christ, then we do not need to fear letting go of our individuality. As we submit to one another, our identity under Christ's Lordship is built up. As Augsburger says, "In a tripolar community, each person's individuality is affirmed (you can be truly you), yet joint participation is achieved (we can be truly we) because at the center we together recognize that God is present (we gather around him)."[21]

---

[21] Augsburger, *Dissident Discipleship, 63.*

I remember having a conversation with a friend a long time ago when I lived in the urban context in South America for a while. I was about to step outside one day to buy the newspaper when he stopped me. "You're going out dressed like that?" he said. I was dressed in an old white t-shirt and that Aussie fashion icon- tracksuit pants (sweat pants). But he felt that I should be better dressed if I was going outdoors. I replied I was only going to get the newspaper. We had an interesting discussion after that which revealed the different cultures that we came from. I was from Australia where we are more relaxed when it comes to what we wear. We wear what we like when we like. However, his culture was more community oriented. People (men and women) made an effort to wear nice things no matter what they were doing because they didn't want to "let the community down." Men and women took pride in their appearance because this meant that a nicer looking community would be fostered. I found that fascinating. No matter what you think about aesthetics or whether you agree with the value that this culture places around beauty, what I found impressive was the awareness that each person had regarding fostering community. They realized that they affected one another. It was not just about the individual but each person keenly observed that the individual was a part of a community and so had responsibilities towards that community.

As we practice *kenosis* and interdependence, we build a community that is strong in mutuality, sacrifice, accountability and service towards each other. Again, this is not always comfortable but I think it is a crucial part of a reign of God community that has the hope of being counter to the values of our world.

Cruciformity, Mutuality (Mission in Reverse) and Peacemaking

Instead of living lives that are permeated by fear, the idolatry of safety and narcissism, what does it look like to live in a cruciform way? Cruciformity, as I have already mentioned means living a "cross-shaped life". It means that there is no room for compartmentalisation as it signifies a life completely surrendered to God. There is no space for a dualism here, which leads to the practice of "Sunday Christianity". This is when as Christians we embody our values as we gather with other Christians however, during the other times, we embody the narratives of our world. Urban spirituality can then, critique some of our consumerist tendencies, which lead us to think about our needs, wants and desires before our neighbour's needs.

I have always admired the way that the Catholic tradition is quite comfortable with the use of the body in worship. There is much more of an ease when it comes to kneeling, prostrating oneself and clasping hands in prayer. I especially love the physical act of crossing oneself. For me this is a symbolic, outward act and a reminder that we are to live cross-shaped lives. I started crossing myself quite naturally one day in prayer as I began thinking about what it means to live a cruciform life. As I prayed, "Lord, let my life be in surrender to you, help me to give up my ego and notice the needs of others today in my daily, mundane acts", I found that my hands were moved instinctively to trace a cross on my body. I have no personal experience of Catholic tradition to learn from, however I remember at the time feeling that it was an important embodied expression of my heartfelt prayer to God. I have since learnt that making the sign of the cross means many things to my Catholic brothers and sisters. It is an act of sanctification, a means of prayer, a display of openness to God and much more. For me, this act of worship can be a reminder of the sacrifice that Jesus made for us and of his ultimate act of kenosis, so we worship. However, the act can also remind us that Christ is not only our Lord who we worship, but he is also the one who we imitate. As I cross myself daily, I am reminded that I step out into the world that day renouncing placing my own needs and wants first, and instead I commit to following in the footsteps of my Lord who thought of others before himself.

Practicing an urban spirituality means living this cruciform existence. In the city where there are so many people in a concentrated space who are different to each other, strangers, tourists, travellers and locals, we need to practice a cruciformity that values surrendering our own rights for the sake and service of others. This will mean practicing a spirituality that is very "ordinary". Often when we think about concepts like surrender, sacrifice and giving up our rights, we picture heroic and grand actions. In the city, however, these concepts are practiced in very mundane, pedestrian and small ways. When I moved into the city, I found that I started to become became more impatient, abrupt and angry. I'm embarrassed to admit this but I saw the change most clearly, as I was driving through inner city traffic every day. Anyone who lives in an urban context understands the frustration of wrestling with the traffic regularly. Of course traffic can be a problem everywhere and many people drive in and out of the city not only locals. But I have discovered that it is a very unique issue in the city and especially if you are negotiating that chaotic context regularly. I try to use my car as little as possible however; I mostly need to use it to go to my workplace three to four times a week in the suburbs. I found that I was becoming more assertive and aggressive in my driving. Instead of allowing others to go first, I would cut in front of them. If others cut in front of me, I would get quite angry that they were taking advantage of me. After some time I realized that, I was changing into a person who was asserting my rights over others continually in the car as I was driving. Urban contexts can this to us. This may seem like an inconsequential and minor illustration however, it is exactly in these kinds of small and ordinary moments that I need to practice cruciformity, a renouncing of my rights in order to show kindness and patience towards others. This is what living a cross-shaped life looks like in urban places where space is contested and tempers flare because of perceived social losses and gains. This spills across to the way that we interact with people on the street, village shopping centers and of course our next-door neighbors.

As I have already noted, this cruciformity also involves understanding power in a different way. Instead of asserting our power, we will be ready to use our power to enable the marginalized. This will sometimes seem as though we are losing our power completely but this is in fact what it means to flesh out a cruciform life. One aspect of this is to practice "mission in reverse." I have already explained this notion from Anthony Gittins book *Bread for the Journey* where he describes his concept of "mission in reverse". Mission in reverse, according to Gittins, means that the people of God are aware that God is not only at work in his church, but also at work in the world. Mission in reverse challenges our usual views and practices of power.

This upside down interpretation of power means that engaging in neighborhood mission looks a little different to how we might have once pictured or thought about it. Mission in reverse means that we not only proclaim, we listen, not only do we invite we also accept, not only do we give we also receive and not only do we teach, we learn. We embody the gospel in our inner city neighborhoods as we serve but we at the same time learn from those we serve. Not only that, more radically, we submit to and surrender to those whom we serve in order to let go of our own strategies and plans and absorb their perspectives. This should be a transformative process for each person or people involved in the mission. As we engage in this practice of sharing and mutuality, each person is transformed, learning from each other as the Spirit of God reveals. This surrender, again, feels like a loss of power in the eyes of the world; however, it is in fact what it means to embody Christ's definition of power.

This practice of cruciformity and mutuality also leads to the practice of peace-making in the neighborhood. As I have mentioned, the inner city neighborhood is a place that can be full of tension due to people being in close proximity to each other who feel as though they are competing for resources. Moreover, the point of this chapter was to highlight the "other" or taking into account that there is diversity, difference and strangeness displayed in the milieu of the inner city. This is wonderful but can also cause tension, as people need to learn to live with each other and accept each other as my example of "Murder Mall" illustrated.

Instead of thinking only at the level of peacekeeping, we can go further and be peacemakers in our contexts. This is an opportunity to practice peace making on a smaller scale. It will again, happen, not on a macro-level though that is possible too, it will happen more on a micro level, that is, in the contexts of our homes, our buildings and our streets. Once we recognise that we are in our neighborhoods in order to serve the needs of others rather than simply maximise our own pleasure, we will be available to bring healing and unity to any situation that may require this. Once we redefine power according to Christ's upside down kingdom, then we are more ready to be reconcilers rather than fighters and bridge builders rather than those who bring more rupture to already tense relationships. This kind of peace-making can take place in mundane events such as driving in the traffic, mediating between warring neighbours, advocating for the poor in a community meeting or providing wisdom in the midst of the sometimes devastating effects of gentrification. Urban spirituality expresses kenotic Christianity in the context of the inner city where the "other" exists. This of course is something that is present everywhere yet in the urban environment it seems to be intensified because a characteristic of cities is that they attract strangers. Diverse ranges of people are drawn to the city because cities are known for the attribute of diversity. An urban spirituality practices cruciformity, mission in reverse and peace making as a way to bless and learn from that environment.

Part Two

Chapter Six:
Putting Urban Spirituality into Practice

The rule for all of us is perfectly simple. Do not waste time bothering whether you 'love' your neighbor; act as if you did. As soon as we do this we find one of the great secrets. When you are behaving as if you loved someone, you will presently come to love him... There is, indeed, one exception. If you do him a good turn, not to please God and obey the law of charity, but to show him what a fine forgiving chap you are, and to put him in your debt, and then sit down to wait for his 'gratitude', you will probably be disappointed.
- CS Lewis

Faith is one foot on the ground, one foot in the air and a queasy feeling in the stomach. - Mother Angelica

Christians tend to love their conferences, books, creeds and discussing the latest theological controversies of the day. This is fine however; it can bias us towards theory, the abstract and conceptual. Talking, reading about theology and attending conferences can help us to mature. However, the emphasis of this book has been embodied practice as a way of bringing authentic transformation to our communities and ourselves. The gospel manifests today through the actions of the local church as people join with God on his mission.

Your neighborhood and mine are supposed to observe their local church there and think "Oh that is what the gospel is. I have heard about it but, *that* is what it looks like in practice." As the gospel is fleshed out or embodied in the local community, we become a witness to a watching world. As people are drawn towards the good news and the attractiveness of Jesus, they join us in the story of the reign of God that we are living out. That is the hope. Often, though, our over focus on right beliefs or theology points to the culture of disembodiment that the Church moves in today; abstract concepts take precedence over our lived-in environment, our doctrine is put in the realm of the sacred but our physical space for instance is not, and as a result we disconnect from much needed embodied engagement in our local neighborhoods.

As urban missionaries, we are the ones who go to places where the gospel must be contextualised in that inner city neighborhood. As we live out the call there to break bread with the poor, welcome the stranger and renounce the idols of certainty and comfort, we embody worship of our God. As this happens, our theology emerges, sometimes in spoken and written words, but always fleshed out in the local community we belong to. In other words, our theology and practice must always be interdependent. As I have mentioned before, this does sometimes tend to birth radical practitioners who are living out a contextual theology in the inner city. As we respond to what the Spirit of God is doing in marginal places which often carry the tensions that I have already outlined in part one, we can become prophets in the inner city who point to the reality and beauty of the presence of the kingdom before our eyes. This is a wonderful thing to behold however; often the broader church cannot understand the methods and practices of these inner city prophets. When God sends the Church prophets, they are usually the oddballs we never expect. These often-perceived "freaks" among God's people embody the radical values of the Kingdom of God. However, we must resist the urge to domesticate them and their message so they look and sound exactly like the dominant narratives of our culture. We would do better to listen, discern and stop being afraid that our theology and practice might be challenged. Can you think of people in your church or context who think outside of the box and are irritants to the existing power structures? We can all think of people like that. I'm not saying all of them are prophets, but I think some perhaps are. The point is to listen to those who challenge the status quo.

In part one of this book, I have shared a theological vision for an urban spirituality. I have suggested that an urban spirituality is at its core a missional spirituality that will be Trinitarian, incarnational, Spirit soaked and kenotic. Nevertheless, of course we can't leave it there. What matters is to be able to flesh out that urban spirituality in our inner city contexts. Each context will be different, however I think that I have made the characteristics of an urban spirituality broad enough that most people living in the inner city will be able to relate in some way. So what does an embodiment of urban spirituality in a local context look like? How do you practice an urban spirituality in your local neighborhood? I will answer the first question in the next chapter on urban spirituality practices. In order to answer the second however, we need to think about the role that habits and spiritual formation play in fleshing out an urban spirituality.

Practices, Habits, and Spiritual Formation

An urban spirituality can emerge as we live in the inner city context. As we experience what I have pointed out are characteristics of the urban environment such as diversity, critical mass, more public spaces and the presence of beauty and strangers, our spirituality is shaped by these marks. We must reflect on what it means to live out and contextualise the story of the kingdom of God in the midst of these urban particulars. This involves designing practices that emerge from an urban context that will express an urban spirituality. These practices are particular to an urban context and need to be designed through the grid of the reign of God in order to join with God's mission in that locality.

However, these urban practices also have the role of shaping and forming us into urban missionaries. As I mentioned in the first chapter, a spirituality that is for missionaries will be a spirituality that is not self-focused and orients the church inwards, but instead shapes Christians to be missional in their community. *Missional* is not primarily about methods rather it is about understanding who we are and our purpose in the world. We are beloved children of God on his mission. The Spirit of God can work through urban spirituality practices in order to shape us into people who will continue to join with God on his mission in our neighborhoods. So mission and discipleship are always linked and feed off each other.

We do not engage with these missional practices or missional spiritual disciplines in order to somehow earn God's favor, they are not ways that we work our way into somehow obtaining merit from God. Rather, they are practices that we engage in so that the Holy Spirit can work through them to shape us and form us into the image of Jesus. I think many people are resistant towards and confused by Spiritual disciplines. Spiritual habits are not a way of earning God's favor or becoming better persons by our own merit. Instead, they are means by which we cooperate with God's work in us. We should see spiritual habits as instruments that the Spirit works through in order to help us continue our conversation with God so we increasingly reflect the image of Christ.

Craig Dykstra says, "Practices of the Christian faith... are not... activities we do to make something spiritual happen in our lives. Nor are they duties we undertake to be obedient to God. Rather they are patterns of communal action that create openings in our lives where the grace, mercy, and presence of God many be made known to us."[1] Then he says, "We don't merely believe our way into spirituality. We must practice our way."[2] This emphasis on practice is crucial because taking action has a sacramental quality. Instead of sitting in the realm of the conceptual, God meets us when we take action. Action has a sacramental component. When we take bold steps to enact the desires that God has placed in our hearts, we encounter him. Simultaneously we realize, that

---

[1] Dorothy Bass and Craig Dykstra, "A Way of Thinking About a Way of Life," in *A Way of Thinking about a Way of Life*, ed. Dorothy Bass (San Fancisco: Jossey-Bass, 2010). Loc 3793
[2] Ibid.

God is already present to meet us but also that he is ready to give us the grace

that we need to do the work that will bring life to our community and world.

While Christian practices or disciplines should always be viewed as missional,

my view is that they have not always been engaged in with this goal in mind. In

Practicing Witness, Benjamin Connor seeks to correct this. He explains:

> Missional theology is a kind of practical theology that explores in every
> aspect of the theological curriculum and praxis of the church the
> implications of the missionary nature of God with the purpose of
> forming congregations to better articulate the gospel and to live
> faithfully their vocation to participate in the ongoing redemptive
> mission of God in a particular context[3]

The emphasis is on the formation of a people who are on God's mission in a

particular context. Connor states that missional theology critiques the

engagement of Christian practices that lead to an inwardness in the church. If

practices are linked to the missional purpose of a congregation, they can shape

people according to that purpose.

However, not all Christians have a positive view of spiritual disciplines or

practices. Many Christians have a "Romantic" view of Christian transformation

and feel that becoming more like Jesus happens automatically because the

Christian has the Holy Spirit. Others have a more legalistic view of practices

that betrays a works based view of salvation. For example, we can sometimes

think that by engaging in prayer, Bible study and church attendance, we are

pleasing God and therefore earning some kind of heavenly rewards. So our

relationship with God is in danger of becoming based on our efforts. However,

instead we need to realise that the Holy Spirit works through these missional

---

3 Benjamin Connor, "Practicing Witness: A Missional Vision of Christian
Practices," (Grand Rapids: Eerdmans, 2011). Kindle Edition. Loc 548.

practices as we engage with them in order to shape us. That means our effort is required in the process of discipleship, it is not as many say "*all* up to God". God brings the transformation as we with effort work with the Spirit so that he can shape us. N.T Wright compares this to learning a new language

> If learning virtue is like learning a language, it is also like acquiring a taste or practicing a musical instrument. None of these "comes naturally' to begin with. When you work at them, though, they begin to feel more and more "natural" until that aspect of your "character" is formed so that at last you attain the hard-won freedom of fluency in the language, happy familiarity with the taste, competence on the instrument.[4]

This formational aspect of missional practices is necessary also because our culture is continually attempting to form us to reflect and live out the false narratives of our world. I have already mentioned various false narratives in part one such as narcissism, individualism, consumerism, to name a few. As we engage in "cultural liturgies", our desires are shaped and as a result, we are shaped according to what we long for. James K.A. Smith explains the role of habits in our lives

> Habits are inscribed in our hearts through bodily practices and rituals that train the heart, as it were, to desire certain ends. This is a non-cognitive sort of training, a kind of education that is shaping us often without our realisation. Different kinds of material practices infuse non-cognitive dispositions and skills in us through ritual and repetition precisely because our hearts (site of habits) are so closely tethered to our bodies. The senses are the portals to the heart, and thus the body is a channel to our core dispositions and identity. Over time, rituals and practices—often in tandem with aesthetic phenomena like pictures and stories—mold and shape our precognitive disposition to the world by training our desires.[5]

---

[4] Tom Wright, *Virtue Reborn* (London: SPCK, 2010), 38.
[5] James KA Smith, *Desiring the Kingdom: Worship, Worldview and Cultural Formation* (Grand Rapids: Baker Academic, 2009), 54.

Our habits train us to long for our heart's desires. If that is true, then our culture is continually training us to love the things of this world, which often run counter to the kingdom of God. However, if we engage in missional practices, then we hope our hearts will be trained to desire to live out the story of the kingdom, welcoming others to join us on God's mission in the local neighborhood.

Urban Spirituality practices express a spirituality that reflects the urban environment from a kingdom of God perspective, however, they also help shape us into missional Christians who reflect the kingdom of God in our local neighborhoods and counter some of the false narratives of our world. This is something that our spiritual mothers and fathers from the past understood very well so we should turn to them at this point for some much needed wisdom, if we want to design practices today that will flesh out a missional spirituality.

Celtic and Benedictine Spirituality

One characteristic of urban spirituality is that it is incarnational. This means that instead of tending towards being gnostic, dualistic and "other-worldly" it is grounded, sees everything as sacred and is very much "this-worldly". All of this stems from the basis of our faith, the worship of God who is other to us, who became like us by putting on flesh in order to show us his love. Therefore, as we think about practices that are incarnational, we can do no better than to take our cue from the ancient Celtics who embodied an incarnational spirituality. Even though their context was not urban, we can learn from their practices and apply this to the inner city because they flesh out an urban spirituality. As they lived out their faith in this way, the Celts embodied the kingdom of God and were a witness to a watching world to the good news of Jesus Christ.

We can see this incarnational spirituality through many of their daily disciplines and habits however one that stands out is the way that they prayed. In *The Celtic Way of Evangelism*, George Hunter points to the prayer lives exemplified by these Christians. Rather than compartmentalizing "life and prayer" as separate aspects of encountering God, they were able to merge the two. Instead of mostly taking breaks for prayer in order to be filled up with God so that the challenges of the day could be met, they prayed during daily activities. Not only that, the prayers were less petitionary and more designed to foster awareness of God's presence in the everyday. This reveals a profound awareness and dependency on the Spirit: they were Christians who listened to the voice of the Holy Spirit in their daily lives. Examples include praying when getting up in the morning, starting the morning fire, bathing or washing clothes or dishes, and going to bed at night. One example for such a prayer for starting the morning fire begins: "I will kindle my fire this morning. In presence of the holy angels of heaven, God kindle Thou my heart within a flame of love to my neighbour, to my foe, to my friend, to my kindred all, to the brave, to the knave, to the thrall"[6]

Hunter says that prayers were prayed for many things:

> ... for sowing seed and harvesting crops; for herding cows, milking cows, or churning butter, for before a meal and after, for a sprain, or a toothache; for a new baby or a new baby chick. Celtic Christians prayed

---

[6] George Hunter, "The Celtic Way of Evangelism: How Christianity Can Reach the West Again," (2010). Kindle Edition. Loc 480.

while weaving, hunting, fishing, cooking or travelling. They knew prayers for the healing of many conditions, including blindness, warts, bruises, swollen breasts, and chest seizures.[7]

This way of practicing spirituality was not only relying on discerning the Spirit in the local context; it was also incarnational in that it was a non-dualistic approach to the practice of Christianity. By connecting with the context and seeing that God was present in the daily things of life, this avoided a dualism that too often surfaced in Western Christianity. In fact, Hunter states that the Celtics would "counsel us to relinquish the illusion that a brief daily devotional each morning, in which (say) people read a snippet of Scripture, a brief reflection and a short prayer... will shape great souls"[8]. Instead of scheduled prayer however many times a day, the Celtic Christians followed the Apostle Paul's encouragement to pray without ceasing. This meant that they practiced praying with their eyes open and did not see it as a secondary kind of prayer but rather equally as valid as praying in retreat with eyes closed. Hunter counsels us today,

> Feel free often to pray with your eyes wide open. Often you have to keep your eyes open when you pray while driving, speaking, attending a meeting or conversing with someone. But praying with one's eyes open is not a regretful necessity of a second-class approach. Closed is not necessarily better than open[9].

Once again, this reveals an incarnational approach to faith as Christians embody the gospel by being present to their local context and aware of the presence of God. As we practice this, we are shaped into God's missionaries in the inner city.

---

[7] Ibid.
[8] Ibid., Loc 1651.
[9] Ibid., Loc 1656.

We can also learn about missional practices for an urban spirituality from the Benedictine movement in the fifth and sixth centuries. The Benedictines did not minister in an urban context, but their practices reflect an urban spirituality as described in this book, which we can apply to our context today.

In *Transforming Mission*, David Bosch says,

> Only monasticism... saved the medieval church from acquiescence, petrification and the loss of its vision and truly revolutionary character... In the midst of a world ruled by the love of self, the monastic communities were a visible sign and preliminary realization of a world ruled by the love of God.[10]

As the monks of the fifth and sixth centuries practiced their missional spirituality, they purified the church from the excesses and privilege of Christendom. They did this by leading exemplary lives for the sake of others, working hard to till the land, taking care of the poor and the peasants who were neglected at that time, and seeking for a just and fair manner of treating the poor in a society where there was little value placed on the marginalized. Bosch concludes, "Although the monastic communities were not intentionally missionary... they were permeated by a missionary dimension."[11] One example of this was St Benedict who established the Rule of Benedict, which focused on guidance for hospitality, rules for work, prayer, interacting with the poor, and character formation. Bosch says, "Precisely because of its profoundly spiritual yet at the same time eminently practical nature, the Benedictine rule has been

---

[10] Bosch, *Transforming Mission: Paradigm Shifts in Theology of Mission*, 230.
[11] Ibid., 233.

one of the most effective linkages of justice, unity and renewal the church has ever known."[12]

The Rule of St Benedict was a way of life for the monks that shaped and formed them into disciples of Jesus. While as Bosch says, movements like these were not explicitly missionary, as they diligently sought to put into practice habits of life to shape their faith, they were a witness to a world that was decaying and showing signs of corruption from the effects of sin. This witness of being light and salt in the world can be a witness to our world and has a missional dimension as people are attracted to the good news of the gospel embodied in the community of Christ. The intent of the monastic community shaped by habits in The Rule of Life was that this would be a community of practicing Christians who lived contrary to the values of the world and this in itself was a witness to the kingdom of God come on the earth. The Benedictine community did not emphasize going out to the world as the Celtic Christians did, however their missional spirituality surfaced especially in the ways that they practiced a Trinitarian, kenotic and incarnational lifestyle through their habits in hospitality, prayer, work and care of the poor.

One practice from The Rule is helpful for developing an urban spirituality around the spiritual discipline of hospitality. It says that any guest who comes into the community must be welcomed with honor and hospitality in the example of Jesus who said, "I was a stranger and you took me in" (Matthew 25:35). The Rule says,

---

[12] Ibid., 234.

When, therefore a guest is announced, let him be met by the Superior and the brethren with every mark of charity. And let them first pray together, and then let them associate with one another in peace. ..In the greeting let all humility be shown to the guests, whether coming or going, with the head bowed down to the whole body prostrate on the ground, let Christ be adored in them as he is also received.[13]

This welcome is given not only to friends of the monks but also the stranger, the marginalized, the poor and the forgotten. In this way, the Rule encourages a practice of seeing Christ in the presence of the poor and vulnerable. The gesture is not only of welcome but also of honor and blessing the other.

The commitment to putting Christian belief into practice rather than allowing it to sit mainly in the mind was an important aspect of Benedictine spirituality, revealing a missional dimension. This is what it means to incarnate the gospel and what it looks like to practice an urban spirituality. Christianity is not simply left as disembodied concept to believe in with the mind, but it is put into practice so that authentic transformation occurs. As this happens, this is a missional witness to a watching world. We can see this through the Benedictine notion of *Conversatio Morum*, which essentially means "the monastic way of life". Terrence Kardong elaborates:

When *coversatio* is used to refer to monasticism, it is mainly the external and tangible element of the life that is in question...it has a connotation of practice rather than theory. To undertake the monastic conversation means that one actually assumes the life patterns of the monk...Concreteness seems to be a vital part of the very origin of the monastic movement. It was the result of the desire on the part of some early Christians to put the teachings of the New Testament into literal practice.[14]

---

[13] *The Rule of St Benedict in English*, ed. Timothy Fry (Collegeville: The Liturgical Press, 1982), 73.
[14] Terrance Kardong, *The Bendictines* (Wilmington: M. Glazier, 1988), 97.

This monastic way of life is especially relevant to the vision of a spirituality for the inner city. This putting into practice or embodying the teachings of the New Testament, especially as we see them expressed in the Sermon on the Mount for example, is essential for a missional spirituality. Rather than a dualism, which fosters a separation of belief and practice, Christians must "incarnate" their beliefs so that the people of God are a living expression of the gospel.

Urban Perspectives from the Majority World

Many large urban centers and cities are in the majority world and from this space; a global urban spirituality emerges that we can learn from as urban missionaries in the West. Not every characteristic can be applied to a Western context, however we can learn from our brothers and sisters in the majority world about living out a missional spirituality in the city. It is difficult to generalize, however we can see a few broad characteristics stemming from the majority world that we can apply to an urban spirituality.

Firstly, many expressions of majority world spirituality focus and prioritise relationships in the way that they live out their faith. In his essay "Spirituality for Asian contexts", George Capaque looks at Filipino culture and spirituality and explains the importance of relationships. He says, "Becoming fully human takes place in the context of the family, the immediate community, and the wider society. Family and community provide the Filipino with a sense of identity as well as a sense of belonging, stability and security."[15] This is quite

---

[15] George Capaque, "Spirituality for Asian Contexts: The Philippines and Beyond," in *Walking with God: Christianity in the Asian Context*, ed. Karen Hollenbeck-Wuest Charles Ringma(Manila: OMF, 2014). Loc 1070.

different to the Western notion of identity that focuses above all things on the individual.

We can learn from a Filipino spirituality, in this case about relationships, in order to temper our Western individualism, which as we have seen, often leads us to loneliness and narcissism. Capaque also says, "Shared identity means that people and harmonious relationships take priority over efficiency and order."[16] If we apply this to what I have said about community and hospitality in previous chapters, this can teach us to learn to focus on others rather than primarily ourselves which can then help us to display a servant-like nature to those we live in close proximity to. Capaque points this out and notices that for Filipinos "Hospitality is a way of life, and a guest is one who comes unannounced, like God. The guest is *atihi*; someone who makes no appointment, but is welcome, like God."[17] This is a beautiful picture of hospitality, welcome and generosity that is shown to family and strangers. I have already identified that hospitality is a much needed practice in urban settings and so I think as we apply this practice, which we can learn from the majority world, we practice the very grace and welcome that God showed to us.

Secondly, majority world spirituality exhibits an increased awareness of the spirit world. This is possibly a key point of difference between Western and global Christianity. Again, without wanting to generalize, we can say however that majority world cultures show a heightened awareness of the spirit world. Capaque highlights this as an aspect of Filipino spirituality that can also be

---

[16] Ibid., Loc 1079.
[17] Ibid., Loc 1087.

applied to other Asian contexts he argues. Since many Asian cultures are very aware of the presence of spirits in the world, often people can have a fear of the spiritual world and feel a need to placate the spiritual world. Capaque says,

> As spirits are part of the Filipino worldview, Filipino spirituality should both affirm and critique this worldview. Christ's victory over 'powers and principalities' at the cross affirms the reality of spirits, but critiques the Filipinos' inordinate fear of offending them and their subservience to them. Among scholars , there is a consensus that 'powers and principalities' point to Pauls' belief in the existence of a plurality of created spiritual powers or forces that 'stand behind' of 'influence' the political life and other areas of human society.[18]

This is an important aspect of urban spirituality that we in the West can learn from simply because of the fact that interest in spirituality is rising. With the increase of fortune telling, visitation to psychics, new age spiritualties and witchcraft for example, now more than ever we need to take the spirit world more seriously. Not only that, we also have to be open to the possibility of God supernaturally intervening in our world. Unless we are cessationists who believe that divine intervention and miracles do not occur today, we must always be open to God' Spirit guiding us and empowering us in ways that do not make sense to our Western logic and rationality. An urban spirituality that ministers in this context of heightened awareness of spiritualties, can glean from our majority world brothers and sisters in this aspect.

Thirdly, majority world spirituality focuses on practicing celebration. This is crucial I think in the inner city where life can sometimes feel mechanized, gray and occasionally overwhelming. Many Christians in the majority world in urban spaces have a discipline whereby they practice celebration even in the midst of life's struggles and difficulties. In their essay "Subversive Urban Spirituality in

---

[18] Ibid., Loc 1122.

Asian Cities" Pascal Bazzell and Amelia Ada-Bucog state that even in the midst

of urban life which can be fast paced and led to a sense of dehumanization, joy

must be a practice that they engage in as a core part of their spirituality. They

say that they organize times of celebrating key events in the life of the often

marginalized and homeless community in order to remind that community that

they are valued members. They suggest, "These gatherings become times for the

community to relax, since most of the live 'hand to mouth' and toil hard for

survival. As people belong to and celebrate with their community, they realize

that they too can be productive citizens of the city and not 'outcasts' as the

'powers-that-be' want them to believe."[19] Practicing celebration is an important

aspect of urban spirituality. As we connect and make friends with those who are

marginalized and as we get to know people who are tired of the city's constant

busyness and stress, celebration is important. An urban spirituality proclaims

the hope we have in Jesus even in the midst of suffering. This is counter to our

culture however; it is the reality of the in-breaking of the kingdom of God in our

world.

Fourthly and alongside this practice of celebrating, there is also an

acknowledgement of suffering as a part of life within the context of majority

world spirituality, especially in urban centers. Many Christians in the majority

world have a better theology of suffering that Westerners do. In the West we get

anxious if we experience pain in our hedonistic culture, however Christians in

---

[19] Amelia Ada-Bucog Pascal Bazzell, "Subversive Urban Spirituality in Asian Cities: Reimagining Spiritual and Missional Practices in Filipino Urban Poor Centres.," in *Walking with God: Chrisitan Spirituality in the Asian Context.*, ed. Karen Hollenbeck-Wuest Charles Ringma (Manila: OMF, 2014). loc 3787.

the majority world understand that pain is a part of life and that God is still present regardless of difficult or overwhelming circumstances.

> Majority world literature reminds us "to serve is to suffer". Discipleship comes at a cost. As Leonardo and Clodovis Boff remind us, Christian often suffer because of their solidarity with he suffering and oppressed and silenced. Christian spirituality and discipleship is forged in suffering. Ajith Fernanado says, "If the Apostle Paul knew fatigue, anger and anxiety in his ministry, what makes us think we can avoid them in ours?"[20]

This acceptance of suffering is necessary for an urban spirituality because living in the city as a missionary, requires sacrifice. Moreover, urban contexts for the reason mentioned in previous chapters are complex places full of congestion, loneliness and stress. We come face to face with a suffering humanity in urban contexts so our theology needs to make room for when God seems silent and distant.

Lastly, many majority world nations teach us in the West what it means to incorporate care for creation in our spirituality. If we are going to practice an incarnational Christianity which values creation, resists Gnosticism and rejects dualism, then dutiful and serious care of the creation is needed. In a gathering, I was speaking at once for pastors, one pastor of a Tongan church in Sydney asked about the environmental crisis that was looming for his people on his island home. His distress conveyed an urgency that I have not normally seen in the Western church. His distress was not only a concern but it was a spiritual crisis for him. This surely must be because many majority world people have cultures that are deeply connected to the land where they live, whereas

---

[20] Graham Hill, *Global Church: Reshaping Our Conversations, Renewing Our Mission, Revitalizing Our Churches*. (Downers Grove: IVP Academic, 2016), 404.

Westerners have, broadly speaking, become disconnected from their land. Gordon Smith says that then,

> "Spiritual formation will mean fostering the capacity to know what it means to be a good steward of creation, as this is inherent in the creation mandate. In turn, this becomes part of our call to justice and righteousness, for we do not exploit resources at the expense of our grandchildren and their grandchildren."[21]

This relates to what I have mentioned regarding and care of our context in the inner city. This notion of creation care or care of our environment is something that often challenges our views of "other-worldly" or disembodied spirituality. Christian spirituality however, must be very "this-worldly" or grounded in place, flesh and working with God now on his mission to restore our world. Smith highlights the problem with a lack of focus on creation or our environment, "When the church discounts the creation, we tend to view the work of the church as otherworldly, and we tend to speak of spirituality as largely interior and personal"[22] This is sadly the way that many Christians practice their spirituality however, an urban spirituality challenges this.

Practicing an Urban Spirituality as a Faith Community and Church Planting

Now that we have considered the marks of an urban spirituality, we must think about what it looks like to practice this in the inner city. As I have already said, as people who believe in the story of the gospel, we need to embody that belief in our neighborhoods in order to be witnesses to this story as well as to be shaped by the story. Stanley Hauerwas says "To be a Christian does not mean

---

[21] Gordon Smith, "Spirituality That Takes Creation Care Seriously " in *Walking with God: Christian Spirituality in the Asian Context*, ed. Karen Hollenbeck-Wuest Charles Ringma (Manila: OMF, 2014). Loc 1959.
[22] Ibid., Loc 2032.

that we are to change the world, but rather that we must live as witnesses to the world that God has changed. We should not be surprised, therefore, if the way we live makes the change visible."[23] Our priority must be then to be witnesses to the world that God has changed. As we live lives that are counter to the false narratives that entangle our world, others will see the beginnings of an alternate world through us; this is the reign of God come in Christ Jesus. So what does it look like to live as witnesses to this changed world in the urban context? What does an urban spirituality look like in practice? In summary of what we have already explored in the first part of this book, we will need to keep these four things in mind.

Firstly, we will need to think about a witness that fleshes out the gospel in the context of the urban environment. This means we need to pay attention to the context of the city so that our theology and practice is contextualized. We have identified the marks of an urban context. Urban contexts are places of diversity and while we might say that in the West this is the case for most neighborhoods, inner-city places thrive on difference. Most urban places have various different sub-cultures existing in the one neighborhood and so face challenges that rural or even suburban contexts might not. Cities are also places that are congested and have high density and this will impact how we flesh out the gospel. Instead of seeing this "critical mass" characteristic of a city as a negative, we must see it as an opportunity to connect with those who live around us. If we want to be witnesses in this kind of environment, what practices will we engage in that will flesh out a Trinitarian Christianity that

---

[23] Stanley Hauerwas, *Brazos Theological Commentray on the Bible: Matthew* (Grand Rapids: Brazos, 2006), 25.

counters some of the challenges and connects with some of the opportunities that come with high density and diversity? Cities are also places that have plenty of public spaces. Many homes are small and so people tend to go out more to gather rather than stay at home. As a result, there are more people outdoors in parks, walking and public spaces are built with this fact in mind. What then would be some practices that we could design which practice an incarnational Christianity that takes physical matter and the environment seriously? The urban context is also a place where beauty can thrive as attention is given through design and art to spaces and buildings for enjoyment and pleasure. However, it can be a place of darkness as we see the effects of stress, loneliness and struggle all congested in small spaces. Where is the Spirit at work in these places? What are some habits that help us to discern what the Spirit is already doing in our neighborhoods through the beauty and darkness that we observe? The city is also a place that has many people moving through it. We can encounter people who are different to us in the city that we might call strangers or those who are "other" to us. What does it look like to develop practices that express a kenotic Christianity which puts others first? Many of these practices might suit a suburban or even rural context also; this is because of the urbanisation of many places in the West. However, these factors that I mention are relevant to and emerge from the distinct characteristics of urban places.

Secondly, we want to think about a witness that focuses on engagement with the world rather than withdrawing from the world. An urban spirituality is going to be missional in the sense that it will focus more on engaging with the community rather than practicing retreat. This is not to suggest that retreat is unimportant because the truth is that we do need time with God away from the business of life in order to grow in our love for God. However, an urban spirituality will be lived out as an "everyday spirituality", it will be a spirituality of the streets, workplace, parks and cafes as we open our eyes to see what God is doing and then join in with his work. Mark Scandrette says

> The term spiritual formation, as it is often used, connotes the practice of solitary introspection, the reading of classic books on prayer or monthly visits to a spiritual director. Interest in these activities... tends to focus, whether intentionally or not, primarily on the interior life of the individual. While the "inner journey" aspects of spiritual formation are obviously important, they must be held in tension with the need for an active, communal pursuit of the way of Jesus.[24]

The practices of an urban spirituality then need to intertwine with the daily activities of people who live and work in the inner city. In this way then, a commute to work could be transformed into an encounter with God; greeting a homeless person on a neighborhood walk could turn into an encounter with the face of Jesus, or a lunch break spent reading scripture in a park could become a striking revelation of God's love for the world.

Thirdly, we need to design several urban spirituality practices that we can engage in regularly for formation and witness. This is where we must take seriously a theology of spiritual formation through habits. Often when I ask people to think about some practices that flesh out a missional spirituality, they will give me examples of programs or events that their faith community might be able to get involved in. This is good of course, but when we talk about habits

---

[24] Mark Scandrette, *Practicing the Way of Jesus: Life Together in the Kingdom of Love*, (Downers Grove: IVP, 2011). Kindle Edition. Loc 901.

and disciplines, we are speaking about set practices that we engage in regularly for formation and witness. In the same way that we look to disciplines such as prayer, Bible reading and church attendance to shape us through the enabling power of the Spirit, we can design practices particular to the urban context which are missional, that will form us and will also tell the story of the kingdom. This means becoming comfortable with the spiritual discipline of repetition which runs counter to the narratives of superficiality, relevance and speed that shape our culture. Essayist and poet Kathleen Norris said this about repetition:

> It is difficult to adults to be so at play with daily tasks in the world. What we do of necessity can drag us down, and all too often the repetitive and familiar becomes not occasions for renewal, but dry, stale, lifeless activity. When washing dishes I am no better that anyone else at converting the drudgery of the work into something better by means of playful abandon. The contemplative in me recognizes the sacred potential in the mundane task, even as the terminally busy go-getter resents the necessity of repetition. But as Soren Kierkegaard reminds us "Repetition is reality and it is the seriousness of life...repetition is the daily bread which satisfies with benediction". Repetition is both as ordinary and necessary as bread, and the very stuff of ecstasy.[25]

Through practicing missional habits, we can discover the ecstasy and spiritual discipline of repetition. As we repeat actions over and over again, we challenge our culture of disembodiment, which tempts us to move on to *the next big thing* quickly before we miss out and become irrelevant. As we repeatedly speak the same words and delight in the same movements, we resist our society that speedily gets bored with the old. In an age of distraction and superficiality, the spiritual discipline of repetition calls us to go deeper. We are beckoned by the

---

[25] Kathleen Norris, *The Quotidian Mysteries: Laundry, Liturgy and "Women's Work"* (Mahwah: Paulist Press, 1998), 28.

Timeless One whispering, "Remember me as you do this. Become like me as you do this. Tell my story as you do this". I experience this often as I engage in various forms of liturgy. Instead of being bored by repeating the same prayers, songs and recitations daily, I feel as though God is establishing me deeper in the Godself every time I engage with the words and practices. As I recite the story of God repeatedly, I am transformed.

Lastly, our witness needs to be communal and so we need to engage in these urban spirituality disciplines as a faith community. We must engage in these practices as a faith community not only individually. If we are going to be Christians that take seriously that our personhood reflects the Three-in-one nature of the Godhead, then we must be intentionally about the practice of our spirituality in community. In my case, I moved into the inner city in order to start a faith community. I did not move in with a team and at first, I lamented this. However, very soon God connected me with friends, some of who were Christian others not, and we were able to engage with some urban spirituality habits in our neighborhood together. I will describe some of these practices in the next chapter. This is important for a spirituality that encourages us in our formation and witness. If you do move into a city neighborhood in order to start a church, I can think of no better way of getting to know the neighborhood and embodying the gospel than to start off by engaging in these urban spirituality practices with your team. Instead of moving into a community and quickly starting up a church service complete with worship pastor, women's ministry coordinator, pastoral care leader and the like, we should be getting to know our community first and listening to the locals. In fact, my opinion is that we should do this for a year or two before we start up what we would normally call church. In this way, we will connect with locals and might even be blessed to see an "indigenous" church community emerge in the local neighborhood. This would be a church community of mainly locals who have shaped and given input to the church style, structure and processes. An excellent start for a church plant would be to move into a neighborhood with a team, engage in urban spirituality practices together and meet regularly for mutual accountability and encouragement for a few years before the gathered and formal aspects of the church take shape.

Now keeping all of this in mind, we turn to the actual practices. These are suggestions only; however, I have found them to be helpful, encouraging and a way that the Holy Spirit has led me on my journey of being an urban missionary with a view to starting a faith community in the city. You might have your own suggested practices to add and develop after reading the first part of this book.

What exactly are the practices that we can engage in which will exhibit an urban spirituality for our formation and witness in the city?

Chapter Seven:
Urban Spirituality Practices

Practice #1 Open-Eyes Prayer in the Neighborhood

Think about what is the first thing you do when someone says, "Let's pray".

Probably like most of us, you bow your head and close your eyes. This is a

bodily expression that shows our inward attitude of humility, reverence and

attention to God. Praying like this is beautiful and right. However, what would

it look like to practice praying with our eyes open in the neighborhood

regularly? This is still a practice that shows reverence for God as we seek God's

presence and activity in the space we live. However, as we pray with our eyes

open, we are engaging in a spiritual discipline which will help us to flesh out a

more incarnational and Spirit-immersed faith, characteristics of an urban

spirituality.

Regularly practicing open-eyes prayer in your neighborhood is an expression of

a spirituality that focuses on engagement and being active, rather than a

spirituality that is more about retreating from the world. When we close our

eyes, go to a private room alone in order to pray this is a good way to connect with God but it can shape our faith to be inward-oriented and sometimes self-focused. I want to quickly add that this isn't always the case, but because Christian spirituality is already biased towards retreat and withdrawal from the world, it can reinforce this inwardness. If we want to counter this and also live out an urban spirituality, we can regularly practice praying with our eyes open. This can mean either being in a public place such as a park or café, looking around our environment and praying as God leads us. Or, and this is what I prefer because God seems to speak to me more clearly when I do this, it can mean prayer walking around the neighborhood. Doing this helps us to discern what God is doing in our urban environment and to become more grounded in our neighborhood.

There is a lot of evidence today about how walking is beneficial for our mind and body. Not only that, walking has a therapeutic effect on us if we feel disoriented by life.[1] Fourth century B.C. Greek philosopher Diogenes came up with the term "it is solved by walking" now commonly expressed, *solvitur ambulando*. Greta Garbo, the famous silver screen actress, said in her in her later years living in New York City,

> When I stopped working, I preferred other activities, many other activities...I would rather be outside walking that to sit inside a theatre and watch a picture moving. Walking is my greatest pleasure...Often I just go where the man in front of me is going. I couldn't survive here if I didn't walk. I couldn't be 24 hours in this apartment. I get out and look at the human beings.[2]

---

[1] Frederic Gros elaborates on the benefits and thoughts around walking in his book *A Philosophy of Walking*, Verso, 2014.
[2] Olivia Laing, *The Lonely City: Adventures in the Art of Being Alone* (NYC: Picador, 2016), 122.

Garbo is vaguely alluding to the fact that walking had some kind of beneficial effect on her. As we move our bodies, observe what we see around us on our stroll and as we connect with the grass, pavement and the street, we feel perhaps more grounded or connected to our environment. It not only helps us process what is going on inwardly, it can help us observe the goings on in our neighborhood. As we do this, I think we can function as cultural exegetes of our inner-city dwellings. Often, as I walk around my neighborhood I see things that bring me a lot of pain, but I also see things that bring me hope and joy. I find out where different sub-cultures gather and I notice who are the locals in the neighborhood. Occasionally it leads to interactions and conversations with my neighbours. The more I walk around my neighborhood praying, the more attached I get to the place. It is almost as through the Spirit is grounding me there through every step I take. The sidewalks bear my footprints and they also become a part of me. I feel "placed". This teaches me that I am tangibly connected to my neighborhood in a very real way and reminds me that the physical is sacred and holy. It also reminds me that the Spirit is present in my neighborhood and at work.

This is why praying as you walk around the neighborhood regularly is a wonderful way to practice discernment of the Spirit. As I walk the streets of my community, I ask God "Lord, where are you at work? Give me your eyes to see the beauty and darkness in my neighborhood. Show me where you are calling me to bless, affirm or challenge in this space where you have placed me." As I walk and talk with God I pray for things that I might never have prayed for as I encounter people, places, buildings, communities and art in my neighborhood that I have not paid enough attention to. Phillip Sheldrake applies Ignatian spirituality to the practice of discerning the Spirit in the city saying, "the key value is a capacity to 'find God in all things'. This implies more than how we are to read our interior 'spiritual' experiences. Rather, it embraces a response to God's action in the processes and challenges of the everyday world."[3] Practicing discerning the Spirit in the neighborhood, shows a faith that is ready to see the inner-city neighborhood as sacred, as a place of God's activity. This spiritual discipline shapes us and it helps us to engage with God's mission. Majority world practitioners also engage in this discipline in the inner city.

> As urban workers, we practice the discipline of open conversation with God in the midst of our conversation with the poor. To practice secret prayer in the street-level context is to pray with our eyes wide open. As with any conversation, we talk to someone with open eyes, but in this case, we intentionally intercede secretly within our hearts.[4]

Regularly practicing praying with eyes open in the city is a way to ground ourselves in our communities and also a way to discern the presence of the Spirit in our urban neighborhood. I have listed some great practical steps by Deb Sternke to follow if you want to practice this discipline on the next page.

---

[3] Sheldrake., *The Spiritual City,* Loc 4311.
[4] Pascal Bazzell, "Subversive Urban Spirituality" Loc 3738.

Practice #2 Neighborliness

In her book *The Lonely City: Adventures in the Art of Being Alone* Olivia Laing

writes

> Imagine standing by a window at night, on the sixth or seventeenth of forty-third floor of a building. The city reveals itself as a set of cells, a hundred thousand windows, some darkened and some flooded with green or white or golden light. Inside. Strangers swim to and fro, attending to the business of their private hours. You can see them, but you can't reach them, and so this commonplace urban phenomenon, available in any city of the world on any night, conveys to even the most

---

[5] http://thev3movement.org/2016/01/one-simple-practice-when-evangelism-completely-freaks-you-out/

social a tremor of lowliness, its uneasy combination of separation and exposure. You can be lonely anywhere, but there is a particular flavor to the loneliness that comes from living in a city, surrounded by millions of people.[6]

Loneliness is an issue in the city even though there are plenty of public spaces that encourage people to go outdoors, and even though the city is a place where people are in close proximity. This is why the Christian discipline of "neighborliness" is a practice that needs to be engaged in regularly by urban dwellers. This means practicing hospitality, which we have looked at as a way of practicing Trinitarian Christianity. Practicing hospitality needs to go further than mere entertainment; instead, we need to practice Trinitarian Christianity. So in the same way that the three persons in the Godhead show welcome towards each other, we must do the same in our neighborhoods. The practice of hospitality caters to the deep need we have for community. It is about getting to know people and befriending those who are in close proximity to us, having the courage to draw close to those who are different to us, and being prepared to allow others to serve and teach us in our neighborhoods.

We need to get to know our next-door neighbors and see this as a spiritual discipline for urban life. I have to confess that like many others, often, I simply want to make my home my sanctuary. I don't want to invite people over or even connect with them after a long busy day at work. I often have to fight the urge I have to nestle at home in front of the TV or a book rather than engage with my neighbors. What I find interesting is that many of us feel this way but at the same time, we crave community. My neighbors lament the fact that we don't

---

[6] Laing. *The Lonely City*, 3.

know the names of people who live right next door to us. However, in order to know names we need to make an effort. We need to be available. We need to be present. Even though I usually resist this, I also find that when I engage with my neighbors I feel more connected and encouraged about my home life. It is not easy to connect, even with those whom we share the same physical spaces in the urban environment. People today, more so than before, are distracted, busy and focused on a screen somewhere so they avoid eye contact. But I have to remind myself when I feel this way that people essentially do want to experience community and connection. Whenever I have made and delivered a gift of food for my neighbors such as spiced Christmas nuts or baked and delivered them to my neighbors, the response and connection has always been better than I anticipated. It usually led to more trust and further friendship. The authors of *The Art of Neighboring* ask, "What good things might happen if you truly got to know the people in your neighborhood and they got to know you?"[7] It's a crucial question and one that we should keep asking ourselves in order to ward off the feeling that most people don't want to connect. My view is that most people do want to relate but we might need to persevere in our acts of hospitality even if we see little progress initially. I have found from experience, that it takes time to build relationships but once people begin to trust, they let down defenses and friendships do form. I have experienced this several time with neighbors.

I also believe that if we are practicing Christian hospitality through neighborliness, we need to pay special attention to the weaker members of our

---

[7] Jay Pathak, *The Art of Neighboring,* Loc 183.

community. We follow the principle in 1 Corinthians 12:23 that tells us to honor the less capable members of the Body of Christ. Living in the inner city means encountering many people every day who are struggling, disoriented and doing it tough in life. In my community, there is a growing tendency to ignore these people. What I'm trying to practice daily as a spiritual discipline is honouring the poor, weak and marginalised as I encounter them every day. This quote from *Untamed Hospitality* by Elizabeth Newman is something I have reflected on to help me in this practice.

> The faithful practice of hospitality must begin and also end with what our society will tend to reject as of little consequence. Waiting for the earthshaking event or the cultural or even ecclesial revolution can paralyze us. We are rather, as the gospel reminds us, called to be faithful in the small things. Hospitality is a practice and discipline that asks us to do what in the world's eyes might seem inconsequential but from the perspective of the gospel is a manifestation of God's kingdom.[8]

As we pay special attention to those who are weaker, more vulnerable and marginalized neighbors in our community, we counter our society's indifference towards these people. More than that, we might come across as "holy fools". Sometimes when we take care of the things and people that others want to marginalize, we receive backlash because we are disturbing the norms in our society. If we are practicing neighborliness in the inner city then this means, reaching out to those who are different to us and showing love in the same way that God the Father, Son and Holy Spirit did when they extended their arms of love to a dying world through the event of the cross. Honoring the weaker members of our society might mean that one day as I'm walking to the bus stop I smile at a person who has been sleeping on the streets instead of avoiding them, or it might mean buying a cup of coffee for that person on a cold

---

[8] Newman, 174.

day, learning their name or getting to know them. Let's bypass the fear that exists in our society of "the other" and instead practice bold risky love in small yet ultimately radical ways.

Practicing neighborliness also means being willing to practice mutuality. We must allow ourselves to receive and not only give. Giving will often put us in the place of the person who actually has something to give, in other words the one with all the power. However, practicing true neighborliness means reciprocity. I have often heard how honored people have felt when I have learned, accepted gifts and received hospitality from them even though they had very little materially to give. Initially I did not want to accept their gifts as I felt that I was taking the little that they had. However, I now freely receive and welcome this blessing. To show honor does not always mean to give but also to receive from those who are usually, and sadly, invisible in our society.

Practice #3 Lectio Missio

I remember one day that I was praying in different parts of my city. I was going on a longer walk than usual and instead of staying in my inner-city neighborhood, I walked for 30 minutes into the heart of the city. There I wandered around the tourist areas and gazed yet again at the familiar landmarks of my city that make it worthwhile for so many visitors over the world to make the long trip. But of course, I'm not a tourist and so even though I think my city is beautiful with its sparkling harbor, near-perfect weather, beautiful parks and stylish buildings, I was that day being drawn to deeper reflection. So I stopped, sat down right on the steps of the Museum of

Contemporary Art where I could gaze at the stunning intersection of nature and the built environment, and took out my Bible. For whatever reason, I turned to the Gospel of Matthew chapter five and started reading the beatitudes:

> *When Jesus saw the crowds, he went up the mountain; and after he sat down, his disciples came to him. Then he began to speak, and taught them, saying:*
> *Blessed are the poor in spirit, for theirs is the kingdom of heaven.*
> *Blessed are those who mourn, for they will be comforted.*
> *Blessed are the meek, for they will inherit the earth.*
> *Blessed are those who hunger and thirst for righteousness, for they will be filled.*
> *Blessed are the merciful, for they will receive mercy.*
> *Blessed are the pure in heart, for they will see God.*
> *Blessed are the peacemakers, for they will be called children of God.*
> *Blessed are those who are persecuted for righteousness' sake, for theirs is the kingdom of heaven.*
> *Blessed are you when people revile you and persecute you and utter all kinds of evil against you falsely on my account. Rejoice and be glad, for your reward is great in heaven, for in the same way they persecuted the prophets who were before you.*

As I read, I looked up and around me. I saw people busily walking to their places of work. I watched shop-owners looking after their business properties, cleaning, serving and exchanging money. For some reason, even though the day was perfect and the scene was tranquil, something uncomfortable began to stir within me. I read the passage again and look up again. "What is it Lord?" I asked. I got some clarity after a while and what I felt the Spirit was highlighting to me was the confronting reality of a rich, prosperous and prideful city that struggles to show gratitude to God for its wealth. I also sensed that this lack of gratitude flowed through to an attitude of indifference towards the weak and struggling in our city. I asked myself, "Is this a place that hungers for righteousness? Is this a city filled with people who are peacemakers? Do we show mercy? Are we poor in spirit?" So the Spirit led me to intercede for my city, to pray for justice, humility and mercy for the poor. I blessed my city.

One way that we can become grounded in our neighborhoods is by reading scripture in a public space. It means that instead of retreating into the quietness of our private rooms, we go outdoors into the cafes, parks and streets of the city, read scripture and think about how the word of God applies to what we see. This not only helps us to practice an incarnational Christianity but also a Spirit-led faith that discerns God's heart for the neighborhood. We become more connected to our place and as we discern God's mission in our neighborhood through his word, we are called to participate with him. We embody the words in scripture rather than simply reading them, or applying them mostly to our "personal" lives. So the reading is not only meant as a devotion, it is a call to change our behaviour and work with God. This is not a purely reflective exercise but one that challenges us to take action. This is similar to the spirituality of the early Anabaptists. Snyder describes Anabaptist spirituality like this:

> It is not in the sense of a systemic 'divine reading' as a means to contemplation (as was practiced in the monasteries) that we may speak of an Anabaptist practice of *lectio divina*... For the Anabaptists, learning, remembering and repeating the words of Scripture was a means to a practical end; it was living the Bible continually that really counted. It was in this sense of learning the Bible in order to live it- and not in the medieval (or modern) sense of a devotional 'exercise in divine reading'- that one may speak of an Anabaptist practice of something like *lectio divina*.[9]

---

[9] C.Arnold Snyder, *Following in the Footsteps of Christ: The Anabaptist Tradition* (London: Darton Longman and Todd, 2004), 116.

As we read scripture in public places regularly, we are shaped by the words we read and we apply them to our surroundings. In this way *missio divina* has an inherent formative and witness-bearing function in a way that traditional *lectio divina* does not. Lloyd Pietersen says

> This approach to reading the Bible assumes that when we come to the text we hear the world of God addressed to us personally. A word that summons us to a response, even if that response is angry questioning! The goal is to come out of such an encounter with the text, changed and equipped for the ongoing journey of becoming more Christlike.[10]

Try these simple steps below and see how you fare practicing *Missio divina* in your local community.

Missio Dei reading

Choose a passage of scripture or follow the lectionary
Find a place to sit and connect with what is going on around you.
Become aware of the sights, sounds, buildings, art and people in that place.
Pray and ask God to show you his heart for where you live.
Read the passage slowly once then look around you
Read the passage again this time connecting with what God is revealing to you about your neighborhood.
Pause and let God speak
Listen to any thoughts and feelings you might have
Read the passage again and then ask God what he wants you to do.
It may be simply to intercede or perhaps take another form of action.

Practice #4 Peace-making

In urban contexts, there is often a striking diversity evident which is not as apparent in many rural or suburban contexts. Different sub-cultures mingle,

---

[10] Lloyd Pietersen, *Reading the Bible after Christendom*, (Milton Keynes: Paternoster, 2011). Kindle Edition. Loc 3258.

instead of a homogenous environment, difference thrives and peppers the cityscape with creativity, a stimulating built environment and a mixture of people representing their particular backgrounds. This is one of the most exciting things about urban life. Tourists and travelers pass through the city and marvel at the art, people and buildings that represent this diversity. Locals also love this creativity and benefit from it as they encounter it daily. However, this wonderful diversity can also be a source of tension and sometimes conflict. The stories I have told of "Murder Mall" and the violent rape of a Lesbian woman in my neighborhood, show tensions between three distinct subcultures in my community; the well-off who have recently moved in, the gay community, and the poor. Each of these groups have their own distinct needs, desires and history which contribute to the diversity of my neighborhood, but which can also conflict with each other. This can create suspicion, fear, and even violence that negatively impacts the whole neighborhood.

We must counter this effect that can tear at the fabric of our local community. One urban spiritual practice we can regularly engage that counters the negative effects of diversity is peace making. Peace making is a discipline we can practice not only in a global sense, but also in smaller, daily ways with those who are in close geographical proximity to us. We may sometimes be called to mediate in conflicts if we become known in our neighborhoods for being ones who practice peace. From disputes between neighbors to speaking healing at local community meetings because of tensions between groups, we can embody this practice as an expression of our urban spirituality.

What does it look like to practice peace making in the city neighborhood? How can we try to mirror the unity that exists in the Godhead and practice a Trinitarian Christianity? The *Celtic Daily Prayer* book reveals that being a peacemaker is not to avoid conflict but to engage in the conflict with a different mindset. It reads "to be a peacemaker is to be a "remedy finder; bridge-builder; breach-repairer; a new-way maker; a relationship broker."[11] Being a peacemaker in the urban context means living a life that promotes *shalom*. *Shalom* is God's vision for the wholeness, healing and reconciliation of our universe. *Shalom* can be practiced in small ways in our neighborhood by functioning as mediators and "relationship brokers" when necessary.

We can create cultures of peace by firstly believing all are made in the image of God. This may seem an obvious point but how many times do we look at those who are different to us and devalue, fear and suspect them instead of seeing the divine spark within? Sometimes the language we use to describe "the other" is unhelpful. I like what my community has done in that instead of calling people "homeless" or other names that can make them seem like problems, we call many of the people in our community "characters". While this term is a little cheeky and points to the quirks of some of the people, it is also a genuinely affectionate expression for those in my community who find it hard to fit into the norms of society. They are people we have come to know, love and receive as part of the one community we live in together with all their blessings and quirks. God is with all of us. Secondly, we practice listening to each other. Deep

---

[11] *Celtic Daily Prayer: From the Northumbria Community* (New York: HarperOne, 2002), 1135.

listening does not come easily in a culture today that is easily distracted, busy and apathetic to the struggles of others. However, we can only truly understand each other when we listen to one another. We can model this as kingdom people and we can also create spaces where we invite different sub-cultures together simply to share and listen. There does not even need to be an immediate outcome in these kinds of gatherings, only a space to share concerns and stories that in effect build trust.

Thirdly, we are to practice permeable boundaries. We practice a "soft difference". As Miroslav Volf explains,

> With such (permeable) boundaries, encounters with others don't serve only to assert our position and claim our territory; they are also occasions to learn and teach, to be enriched and to enrich, to come to new agreements and maybe reinforce the old ones, and to dream up new possibilities and explore new paths. This kind of permeability of religious individuals and communities when they engage one another presupposes a basically positive attitude toward the other- an attitude in sync with the command to love the neighbour and, perhaps especially, to love the enemy.[12]

It is not easy to practice permeable boundaries in a world that increasingly values polarization. It seems that more and more we hear from voices that betray a "drawing a line in the sand" attitude. Our world values an "if you are not with me then you are against me" posture. Instead, I think that today those who adopt a position from the center will be the wise ones who mediate and bring healing to conflict situations in our neighborhoods. In a sense, this is what it means to practice *kenosis*. This does not mean losing our identity or

---

[12] Miroslav Volf, *A Public Faith: How Followers of Christ Should Serve the Common Good* (Grand Rapids: Brazos, 2011), 133.

compromising on the things we value, but it does mean a gentler and more conciliatory posture of submission.

Fourthly, we seek common ground. There may be times where there is evil present and we must resist this completely. However, usually in situations where different sub-cultures are at tensions with each other, both parties can find some kind of common ground. For instance, gentrification is occurring in my neighborhood, which highlights the tensions between locals and newcomers, poor and well to do. Surely, this is an opportunity to try to find some common ground so that we live together not only without conflict, but also even by developing friendships between the different sub-cultures. The goal is not merely lack of conflict but instead to also strive for wholeness and thriving of each subculture in the community. Can we dare to become friends with those who are very different to us?

Fifthly, to be peacemakers we practice forgiveness. Inevitably, people will be hurt in a world that is broken and full of people competing with different desires and needs. One example in my community is the tension that exists between the local community and the state government. The government is building a light rail that will cut through our inner city community and one consequence among many, is that many very old beloved trees are being cut down. There is a lot of anger in my community about this. I feel angry just writing about it. How can I be someone who practices forgiveness rather than inciting further hatred towards the government? Sometimes we will have to model forgiveness first even if our hearts beat as one with the same concerns of the people in our neighborhood. A while ago some of us at our neighborhood center ran a course that helped people practice happiness and thriving. We taught disciplines such as gratitude, kindness, being thankful, self-care and forgiveness. One day we shared as part of this course our stories of practicing forgiveness towards each other. The people, who shared the stories, read the poignant and profound accounts of people practicing forgiveness, sometimes in difficult circumstances, and they were moved by the stories. Doing these kinds of activities can help create a culture of peace making in the community.

Practice #5 Slow in the City

I walked into the meeting room and there were already several people sitting down in concentric circles. Some had their eyes closed, others were looking around, but everyone was silent. I took my seat on the hard wooden bench and scanned the room again. It was a very simple room, evidence of a frugal ethic. There was one perfectly styled floral arrangement in the outer circle. The floorboards were polished and shone in the light that came through the windows. I had been given brief instructions as I walked in and I began to read them. They encouraged me to be silent and focus my thoughts, reflect and to not rush to speak. So I folded up the instructions, shut my eyes and sat still in the room for about an hour. I noticed my breathing, I heard occasional stomach rumblings and people scratching, sniffing or clearing their throats. I listened to the sound of the distant traffic outside and shouts from people on the street. It seemed so busy outside yet so still inside the room. I felt my body slow down and a restlessness within me settle. After about an hour of silence only broken by one woman who stood up to briefly share about her sick sister, someone got up, shook hands with the person next to him and with that the meeting was over.

You might have realized the meeting that I was attending was a Quaker gathering. Only a ten-minute walk from my home in the inner city, there is a Quaker building with a sign out the front that reads "Society of Friends". That day when I attended their weekly gathering, I learned about the discipline of slowing down in the midst of a busy urban context. I remember thinking in that meeting room how odd and counter-cultural it was to have a group of people sitting in a room, still and silent when there was busyness, speed and stressed people only a few meters outside the door on the streets of my neighborhood. It made me realize that often we adapt too easily to the narratives of efficiency, pragmatism and our results driven culture. We need to stand against the aspects of our culture that dehumanize us and turn us into machines rather than people who need rest and renewal. In the city, there is congestion and tensions because of the different sub-cultures that exist side by side. Fast-paced attitudes and practices can lead to depletion, and so we need to practice a slowing down in order to reconnect with God, one another and our urban environment. This doesn't necessarily always mean retreating to the mountains, hills and beaches to reflect in nature in order to remove ourselves from the negative effects of the city. Certainly, this is a good practice. But what about we ask ourselves what it might look like to practice slowing down in the midst of our urban environment? As we do this, we model God's Sabbath and a restored humanity. We stand against the dehumanizing forces in our society.

We can find the sacred spaces in our city and practice rest. In the city, there are places that people go to in order to stop, reflect, eat and slow down. They are usually parks or places that are beautified by nature. Sometimes these sacred spaces can be buildings or monuments that hold special significance for the community. Sheldrake says, "Although for some people protected domestic spaces are particularly sacred, it is interesting that many common responses point to various forms of public place. Two that are regularly mentioned in discussions are natural places such as parks, lakes or rivers and art galleries or museums"[13] The fact that many people in the city would say that they find sacred spaces in public places such as parks, shows a different view of spirituality which embraces community rather than solitude. Rest in the urban space is crucial. Rest is just as important to God as work. It's our society that has valued work over rest. Busyness has become an idol. But in God's economy, they are both equally crucial for humanity to thrive. When we live without proper rest, we become less than human. We become like machines, we absorb our predominant cultural narrative without critiquing it. And so when we join with God on his mission without perceiving rest as vital, we are behaving as though we are less than human. Doing mission in the way of Jesus ought to be an essentially restful work.

We can practice also patience and restraint to slow down in the city. What does it mean to wait in a culture of instant gratification? How do we resist our society's constant search for bigger, better and more? We must practice savouring the moment, noticing the ordinary things that usually go unnoticed

---

[13] Sheldrake., Loc 3157.

and even practicing "ordinariness" in a culture that worships showiness and status. Chris Smith in Slow Church says, "Patience, as Nouwen, McNeill and Morrison explain, can be understood as a third way between the polar extremes of fight and flight. In patience, we learn to abide in each particular moment, finding it not empty but rather full of the grace of God. How do we grow deeper into our calling as the patient people of God when our surroundings reinforce our inner restlessness?"[14] Sometimes this might mean saying no to the things that others freely accept into their busy lives. It might mean more flexible boundaries around our time rather than tight schedules that leave no margin for rest, divine interruptions or play. Slowing down in the midst of city living is a counter-cultural and culture shaping practice that renews our mission and simultaneously embodies it.

Practice #6 Celebration

I have just returned from my local neighborhood center Christmas party. There I sat at a table with people from a variety of backgrounds and felt a little privileged surrounded by some people who had it tough in life. One lovely person told me that he was having a "quiet Christmas" this year. And the table was silent when I spoke about all the shops having such wonderful things to buy for presents this year. I began to check myself when conversing to make sure that I didn't make assumptions about how they would spend Christmas and whether they could afford to buy many gifts or not. I looked around me and saw about a hundred people who looked like they came from all walks of life. There

---

[14] John Pattison and Christopher Smith, *Slow Church: Cultivating Community in the Patient Way of Jesus*, (Downers Grove: Intervarsity Press, 2014). Kindle Edition. Loc 1109.

were the well off, the strugglers, dancers, knitters, the elderly, the unwell, the volunteers, immigrants, refugees, all the people who make up my local neighborhood center. We sat together and were treated to a magnificent three-course lunch. The room was decorated and the Christmas tree was up, the staff encouraged people to dance as the entertainment, a local drag queen, sang his heart out to *I will Survive* and *Love is in the Air*. Everyone was enjoying himself or herself. As I walked back to my home, the children at the school across the road from my home were outside at their last assembly for the year accepting their awards. Cheers, applause and laughter were heard and heartily shared as each child came up to receive a commendation for a year of hard work.

Celebration in the midst of difficulty is a spiritual practice. It is crucial to practice joy in a world that is broken and leaves us feeling devastated so often. In the urban context where there are people who are marginalized, with mental illness and those who are lonely, even more necessary then is the habit of laughter, and joy in the face of hardship. We practice this joy not because we are avoiding reality or sticking our heads in the sand in order to avoid confronting present circumstances. We engage in this deep joy because of our theology. We believe that when Jesus came into our world, through his death and resurrection the cosmos was transformed. We now live in the "in between" time when we have experienced a taste of the kingdom but we wait for its full consummation at the return of Jesus. So our joy is that the kingdom is already here and the powers of death have been defeated. Our joy is in the hope that one day our world will be perfect. There will one day no longer be loneliness, heartache, sickness, abuse, and death and our joy, only partial today, will be complete in the future, as we gaze into the loving face of Jesus for the first time.

> The resurrection of Jesus relieves us of the fear of death. "Where oh death, is your victory? Where, O death is your sting? (1 Cor. 15:55). But the fuller story of the New Testament is that God's people have been resurrected as the body of Christ. Just as Jesus is the embodiment of the *shalom* that God intends for creation, the church's role in the drama of creation is likewise to be the embodiment of God's *shalom*, albeit in a form that hasn't yet been fully realized.[15]

Even though many people live lives that exhibit signs of despair, death and sickness, we can, without being glib or insensitive, encourage joy as a sign of our present and future hope in the full expression of the kingdom.

How do we practice this joy? People who minister in the context of the urban poor know the importance of the discipline of joy in the midst of suffering.

> When we serve among those who are living on the periphery of the city, we need spiritual disciplines that will sustain God's peace in out hears so that we don't become overwhelmed by their desperation and hopelessness. As we wrestle with our own feelings of inadequacy because the help we provided seems like a "drop in the bucket", we may be tempted to quit even before we try to reach out.[16]

They note that because marginalized people may struggle to celebrate, there is more reason to practice the spiritual discipline of joy. Therefore, "life passages such as birthdays, baby dedications, weddings, and Christmas are reasons to gather for simple celebrations, where we can express gratitude for the gift of life God has given to us."[17]

---

[15] Ibid., *Slow Church,* Loc 418.
[16] Pascal Bazzell., *Walking with God,* Loc 3795.
[17] Ibid., Loc 3779.

The discipline of joy in the midst of suffering and struggle is not difficult in terms of being creative in practicing this discipline. The celebrations need not be difficult or laborious. Often celebrations and parties become so elaborate that the organizers are exhausted and dread planning further events. Simple practices such as commemorating birthdays and special events of those who are not used to celebrating, thinking of those who will be alone at important times of the year such as holidays and Christmas, sending cards to commemorate small steps towards transformation, can all bring joy in a community even in the midst of pain. There are many ways that we can practice joy. We will also need to be people who practice joy daily if we want to model this to others. I like Tan's term "thin slices of joy"[18] which reminds us that we need to daily practice finding the joy in all circumstances and celebrating ordinary events. This builds our capacity for more joy in the future. Our minds have been so wired for despair in our world; we need habits of joy in our lives that help us to live as the fragrance of another reality that has already entered our world today.

Practice #7 Re-enchantment

I described in an earlier chapter the horrific story of a woman who was brutally raped in a laneway in my neighborhood and the way that the community decided to place a work of art there that stood as a reminder of the terrible act. This was a stand that the community took in order to proclaim that our neighborhood rejects such acts of violence. It was a warning, an expression of grief and a strong statement of repudiation all at the same time. Many people walk past that laneway every day and also go there intentionally to remember

---

[18] Chade-Meng Tan, *Joy on Demand: The Art of Discovering the Happiness Within* (New York: Harper Collins, 2016), 111.

what happened, sympathize with victims of violence and then make a commitment to reject that violence. That space has become sacred in my community.

How do we discern the sacred spaces in our community? This will mean discerning the presence of the Spirit in the neighborhood. If we believe that God is at work there and we take an incarnational approach, then we will be thinking about practices of re-enchantment, which will help us to connect with God's presence outside the confines of the church. It will mean finding the sacred spaces and identifying with people's longings then reflecting on how the reign of God narrative can bring restoration to those longings.

Charles Taylor, in *A Secular Age,* argued that as a result of the Enlightenment, the West now existed in a state of 'disenchantment' whereby everything sacred has virtually been removed from the daily stuff of life. He says

> The presence of something beyond (what we call today) the 'natural' is more palpable and immediate, one might say physical, in an enchanted age. The sacred in the strong sense, which marks out certain people, times, places and actions, in distinctions to all others as profane, is by its very nature localizable, and its place is clearly marked out in ritual and sacred geography. This is what we sense and often regret the passing of, when we contemplate the medieval cathedral.[19]

However, if we have eyes to see, we can discern many examples of re-enchantment in the city. The difference though, is that sacred space is often not experienced in the cathedrals, churches and other normally "holy" places in the urban context. Instead, it's on the streets, lanes, alleyways, cafes, pubs and bars of the city. Christendom gave us cathedrals as sacred spaces in contrast to the

---

[19] Taylor, 553.

profane, but in a society that is post-Christendom, we more clearly see that the sacred spills out onto the streets, mixing with the horror and beauty of humanity. This means a radical shift in the way that we normally delineate between sacred and secular. Madeleine L'Engle has said, "There is nothing so secular that it cannot be sacred, and that is one of the deepest messages of the Incarnation."[20] If we are guaranteed then that our neighborhood ground is sacred, how do we work with God there?

In Phillip Sheldrake's book *The Spiritual City: Theology, Spirituality and the Urban*, he offers this insight:

> Re-enchantment seeks to make public space more than a context for human socialization created purely by consumerism or tourism. Rather, we should work imaginatively and experimentally with public space to make it the medium for a transformation of imagination and behavior through protest gatherings (non-legislative politics), art, education and entertainment.[21]

So practices of re-enchantment involve firstly, discerning the presence of the Spirit and this is done through engaging in some of the practices already mentioned such as prayer walking and *lectio missio*. Secondly, it then means working in public spaces for transformation as Sheldrake points out. This is very close to the practice of place-making which we will look at next. As we pray with our eyes open in our neighborhood and we read scripture from a missional perspective, we will begin to engage in a process of cultural exegesis that is led by the Spirit. Often this will lead us to research the stories and memories that

---

[20] Madeleine L'Engle, *Walking on Water: Reflections of Faith and Art* (Colorado Springs: WaterBrook, 2001), 51.
[21] Sheldrake, *The Spiritual City*, Loc 375.

rest in our neighborhoods. This is an insight into the way God worked in the past in those places and also indicates how he will work in the future.

As we research into the stories of our community, this will certainly involve hearing the stories of those who have lived in our neighborhood for many years. These people who are locals can tell stories of the changes that have occurred and will give us insights into their longings. One example from my community is an art project called Village Voices that was run by Action Research Performer Astra Howard for a season in my neighborhood. This project fused action-research, cultural exegesis, art and place-making by asking people to contribute their stories about our neighbouhood at various workshops run in several places. People's stories were crafted by Howard and then displayed on a large, mounted dark panel in a small, narrow laneway in my community. The words were white, large and illuminated so that the artwork would get the attention of all passers-by. One person's story read:

> Terra Australis La Dolce Vita
> Philanthropy Behind Terrace
> Doors Luxury Abandoned
> You Now a Stranger In The
> Mirror Gentrified Hipsters
> Are Obsolescence In Waiting[22]

This might not mean very much to those outside my community however, anyone who lives in my inner-city village will realise that this poem is revealing what many locals think about the gentrification that is rapidly occurring in my urban context.

---

[22] http://astrahoward.com/project-history/2016/village-voices/village-voices/village-voices-17.html

This is a wonderful example of cultural exegesis and secondly of creating a space that is for reflection and has the potential to bring transformation. In the midst of a busy space, passers-by are challenged by the words in the alleyway. The work is a reflection of the community and a "sacred space" which encourages the onlooker to look deeper at their community. We must then ask, what is the Spirit saying here? What does God have to say about urbanization and gentrification? Gerald Wilson says that the psalms for instance have a lot to say to us about place and loss: "Psalm 137 reflects the agony associated with the loss of place and identity and the lack of concern or understanding displayed by majority culture. Psalm 12 describes the tyranny of articulate speech by which slick, effective speakers oppress and manipulate those unable to counter their arguments."[23] As we pray and read scripture, God shows us the longings of our community and then helps us to take action to create places that are re-enchanted for the betterment of our cities.

Practice #8 Place-making

Place-making is not a new idea. It gained traction in the 1960's with Jane Jacobs book *The Death and Life of Great American Cities* where she radically stated that cities should not only be places for cars and consumerism but also for people. The idea behind place-making is to engage in community consultation when designing new spaces, buildings and events so that the surroundings become "humanized". Jacobs says, "Cities have the capability of

---

[23] Gerald Wilson, "Songs for the City: Interpreting Biblical Psalms in an Urban Context," In *Psalms and Practice: Worship, Virtue and Authority* (Minnesota: Michael Glazier, 2001), 235.

providing something for everybody, only because, and only when, they are created by everybody."[24] She also coined the term "Eyes on the street" which meant that locals were to contribute to a safe and vibrant city neighborhood by paying attention to the happenings on the streets of where they live. This concept of eyes on the streets means that local are able to watch, be amused by and participate in the "street ballet" that occurs on city streets. This is of course an evocative description of the varied and wonderful yet sometimes messy interaction between people, animals, bikes and cars on the neighborhood streets. Jacobs imagined that, "The ballet of the good city sidewalk never repeats itself from place to place and in any one place is always replete with new improvisations." [25] If this is true then how much more should we be asking the Spirit to show us how to enter into that "ballet of the streets" in order to discern the mission of God? If there is continuity between this world and the next as I have argued, then it is our responsibility and privilege to be place makers in our local neighborhoods redeeming what is needed and affirming what already exists that is good, just and true. In every sense, place-making is about beatifying, engaging with and contributing to the local city neighborhood for its good.

I think place-making can be an incarnational practice that is expressive of an urban spirituality. Place-making involves discernment, creativity, and community voices being heard in order to design and contribute to a better city. This means that we have very firmly in our minds the vision of a good city that

[24] Jane Jacobs, *The Death and Life of American Cities* (New York: Vintage reissue edition, 1992), 238.
[25] Ibid., 50.

points to the narrative of the kingdom and we work with God in our context for that vision to eventuate. We know that this vision will only be complete at the consummation of all things in Christ; however, today we labor with God doing his work. Sheldrake says that a report on *Faithful Cities* discovered that "the good city is person-centred rather than shaped by abstract approaches to politics, planning and structural efficiency."[26] He summarises Richard Rogers in the Reith Lectures and says that a good city should be just, beautiful, creative, ecological and diverse.[27] This involves not only proclaiming the gospel but also embodying it by serving in our neighborhoods to make the place just, beautiful and good. This is a call that Christian designers, architects and urbanists need to take seriously. What is the vision of "the good city" God would have for your city neighborhood once you tell the story of the kingdom of God in that place?

Many Christians are not yet comfortable with seeing place-making as a spiritual discipline. It somehow does not seem equal to prayer, Bible reading and church attendance. This is evidence of an unhelpful other-worldly spirituality and reveals the dichotomy we make between the sacred and the secular. As a result, the best way of practicing place-making today I find, is to be involved with local community groups and councils that engage the community for consultation as they make or remake public spaces. We need to see this as a missional discipline. This means making time to attend local council meetings and rallies in order to participate with community decision-making. Often, we are more comfortable attending events that are to do with broader values such as justice

---

[26] Sheldrake, Loc 385.
[27] Ibid., Loc 4266.

and peace; however, we rarely apply this thinking to activism in our local neighborhoods. It seems again, the ordinary and the mundane are sidelined in our Christian practice for the bigger and more spectacular. I often attend council meetings and other gatherings advertised, in order to contribute to discussions and see if there is any way that I can serve. I view this as a spiritual discipline.

My local neighborhood center runs many consultations in order to discern what the community needs and wants and then the center leadership thinks about ways to implement these ideas if possible. I am on the board of my neighborhood center and love listening to the thoughts and ideas of my community. I once ran a course at this neighborhood center, which involved discussions around happiness, and so I set up a blackboard a few times at the local markets and asked people to write on the board what happiness meant to them. I was able to discern the longings of my community through this practice. One time, at the end of the day when engaging with people in this way, I laughed and grieved at the many different expressions of happiness that exist in my community. People shared what makes them happy and examples were: dogs, trees, to be with lovers, getting straight As, gin and tonic, avocado on toast, family, fulfilling dreams, telling a good joke, being in the now, not (about) getting more than 40 likes on Facebook, clarity and more! I needed to pray at the end of the day that God would redeem and bless whatever he needed to. When I participated in the already mentioned Village Voices workshop, I was able to present a story that embodied some of the yearnings of my neighborhood. My work that was displayed in the narrow, dark alleyway wall of my neighborhood on a panel in bright large letters read,

> I was Afraid of Making Eye
> Contact This City Can Amplify
> Loneliness Character runs
> Far Deeper A Gaze that
> Starts a Conversation
> I wanted to be a Local[28]

I remember visiting the laneway frequently and seeing homeless people sleeping next to the sign, others walking past looking down at their phones not noticing either the poem or the poor person sleeping by its side. However, often when I walked through the alleyway I noticed people reading the work and taking photos of it. Some of them would smile as they read it. I saw several posts on social media from people I did not know sharing the poem with hashtags such as "meaningful" and "deep". I felt as though I had not only expressed some of the sadness in my community but also contributed to creating a transformative space that can make room for reflection and even action in order to create a better city. Viewing place-making as a spiritual discipline is new to the Christian mindset but it reveals an urban spirituality that is incarnational, discerning and embodies a vision of the kingdom in our community.

Practice #9 Civility

One year on Christmas morning, I was walking to one of my local churches trying to make sure I got to the service on time. As I walked along the streets of my neighborhood I greeted some people mostly tourists, joggers and homeless,

---

[28] http://astrahoward.com/project-history/2016/village-voices/village-voices/village-voices-17.html

with a smile. Some people ventured a "Merry Christmas" and I replied with a Christmas greeting. As I got closer to church, I noticed a disheveled looking older man lying by the side of the road near a shop. His eyes were closed. He had a backpack next to him and a blanket pulled around him. However, what stood out to me was his face. His face was deathly pale and he was unnaturally still. It looked like he wasn't breathing. His pale face stood out so much that others who walked past also stared at him. We are used to seeing people sleeping on the streets in my neighborhood but you get to know what looks "normal" and what does not. Most people were too scared to draw too close to him. However, I felt I could not walk past without checking on him. So I drew a little closer and noticed that he seemed to be breathing and alive. I have to admit that I was not 100 percent sure about this as I left him, but I felt comfortable enough, even if also a little guilty, to keep walking to church. I made a note to make sure to walk the same way on the way back and check on him again. After church, I walked past him and saw that he had moved a little and there were in fact signs of life. I felt a massive sense of relief about having avoided a horrible start to Christmas Day and of course more importantly, that this man was alive!

That kind of thing happens to me often as I engage with my neighborhood. It's not always about looking out for those who have it rough in life, but as I notice the regular rhythms of my community, I can distinguish when something is out of order or at least simply just needs attention. This seems to be partly what Jane Jacobs meant when she coined the term "eyes on the street". There is a sense in that phrase that being a good citizen meant noticing what goes on in your neighborhood and then stepping in to help or contribute when necessary. I would call this the spiritual practice of civility. It means taking on board that old-fashioned sounding notion of being a "good citizen" seriously and even seeing it as a spiritual practice. No matter what our circumstances are in the neighborhoods we live in, we can all do this. God's message to the exiles in Babylon was to "Seek the peace and prosperity of the city to which I have carried you into exile. Pray to the Lord for it, because if it prospers, you too will prosper" (Jeremiah 29:7). This is the practice of civility. To seek *shalom*, peace, justice and compassion in our city is to embody God's mission there. Again, this is an incarnational practice that some might struggle with because it may not be perceived as "spiritual' enough. However, my view is that it expresses an urban spirituality that embodies our faith in our local communities. Usually, practicing civility does not earn us many accolades; however, it does connect us to our neighborhood and to the people who live there as we engage in the daily, mundane and ordinary life of a good citizen there. It is evidence of embodied love shown to the people who we are the closest to geographically. As we do this, we contribute to the good of our neighborhood and make them places of *shalom*.

Jacobsen defines civility as "the formal politeness that results from observing social conventions."[29] He laments the fact that we are becoming less and less civil towards one another and says, "Therefore, while it may seem a laughably small place to start, one place to begin increasing the safety of our cities may be

---

[29] Jacobsen, *Sidewalks in the Kingdom*, Loc 2504.

in the simple act of relearning the practice of civility."[30] I would add that this practice is not only about safety but also a broader vision of embodying God's shalom.

There are various ways that you can practice the discipline of civility in the inner city neighborhood. There are some that I try to live out daily. One example is I make time to attend local community or council meetings. My community often has small gatherings in community centers, parks and other places depending on the event, in order to give and receive communication about various neighborhood projects. One recent meeting was an opportunity for our local mayor to convey to us feedback about a light rail project that is disorienting my community quite a lot. The mayor asked that we would meet at a local park that would be significantly affected. I went to that meeting not only because I want to know if my street would be affected detrimentally, but also because I felt that it was my responsibility to engage with my community and the leadership of that community.

Another practice could be to join the board of a local community center or other groups that make a substantial contribution to the neighborhood. I have joined the board of my local community center and see it as my way of serving that community. Often as Christians, we quickly step up to be on church boards and pay scant attention to the neighborhood committees that need the practice of *shalom* there through us. As a practice of civility, I try to make sure that I pay special honor to the weaker members of my community. This is not always easy

---

[30] Ibid., Loc 2516.

and I think we sometimes romanticise poverty in the West. Our duty and spiritual practice is to honor the weak and vulnerable around us. This means learning people's names for instance rather than describing them as "the homeless" and engaging in conversation with them when we see the opportunity. This goes beyond giving money or doing "charity" work. Instead, it is about treating those who make up part of our community with honour and respect despite their physical appearance or their social status. There are many other ways that we can practice civility and each will be different according to our contexts; however, it is I think a crucial expression of an urban spirituality and of an enfleshed faith.

Conclusion:
Living Holy in the City

Be assured that from the first day we heard of you, we haven't stopped praying for you, asking God to give you wise minds and spirits attuned to his will, and so acquire a thorough understanding of the ways in which God works. We pray that you'll live well for the Master, making him proud of you as you work hard in his orchard. As you learn more and more how God works, you will learn how to do your work. We pray that you'll have the strength to stick it out over the long haul—not the grim strength of gritting your teeth but the glory-strength God gives. It is strength that endures the unendurable and spills over into joy, thanking the Father who makes us strong enough to take part in everything bright and beautiful that he has for us. - Colossians 1:9-12

The Church has shut its doors

I woke up early one Sunday morning on a bright, brisk wintery day to attend the worship service of a neighborhood church. Most churches in my neighborhood, as with many inner-city churches, are long established and have beautiful buildings. This one was no exception. As I walked to the church, I reflected on the age of this church, the history that it contained and how majestic the building was. There is very little chance of new churches being given space in the inner city or being able to afford the land. I also thought about how much I love walking to a local church. I strolled past the cafes that I frequented regularly and took time to notice the public housing nearby as well as the road works that were happening. I felt grounded in my place, it was my home and it felt right to be going to worship in a community that had emerged from that context.

I finally got to the grand old building and I was looking forward to getting a little warmer inside. As I walked past the plaques dedicating the building to those who had established the church, I pushed open the creaky old gate and walked up the heavy stairs towards the big wooden doors. Surprisingly the doors were shut. "Maybe they are just trying to keep warm," I thought to myself. So I knocked softly at first. No answer. I knocked harder. Still, no answer. I looked at the time. I had come five minutes late. I wondered if I had got the time wrong. I stood there feeling a little frustrated wondering what to do next. Maybe there was another entrance. So I walked around the building twice to try to look for some kind of opening, but found nothing. By this stage, I was getting upset. I walked back up the stairs that I had climbed already and knocked very loudly on the door. Again no answer. I put my ear to the door and could barely hear organ music playing in the background. At this stage, two of my friends who also lived in my neighborhood had come along to the worship service. All of us banged at the door loudly and walked around the building again without success. We sat on the stairs and I wondered about how ridiculous the situation was. It was laughable. Finally, we heard sounds at the door and then it opened. A little old lady peered through from the other side "Oh I'm terribly sorry" she said, "The wind must have shut the doors. Please come in." We walked in, sat on the pews of this church, and joined in the singing with the ten to fifteen others who were also there.

Afterwards, the event stayed with me. I felt a deep frustration and grief developing in me about what had happened. It seemed to me to be a kind of sad illustration and even a prophecy for what was happening with the Church in my neighborhood. There was a sense in me that the Church had retreated from the world, become irrelevant and stale. I felt like the buildings were old and beautiful but that the Church had become a relic of the past. Even though I might be the only one in my neighborhood literally beating down the doors of the Church trying to get in, it was still an illustration for me of the longings, needs and opportunities in my neighborhood that are not being met by the Church. People need the gospel, they need to hear the story of the kingdom, yet the Church has withdrawn from society and shut its doors.

God is at work in the inner-city neighborhood, God is at work through the people of God, the churches, in the neighborhood. I know this is true. However, the Church needs to more intentionally move away from being internally focused and look to the place in which it exists to join with God on his mission there. Darrell Guder has said "The preservation of the institutional church as we have known it is not the purpose of the gospel."[1] It is true that often, the Church gets caught up in internal machinations and forgets that the gospel is about the restoration and reconciliation of the universe. God has created the church to accomplish his purposes of restoration. The church is not an end in itself. This is something that we can especially apply to the urban context in the West, which sits deeper in post-Christendom, and many churches there seem to be struggling with relevancy.

---

[1] Darrell Guder, "Worthy Living: Work and Witness from the Perspective of Missional Church Theology," *Word and World* 25, no. 4 (Fall 2005): 427.

One day I was speaking with a local café owner. She asked me what I did for a living and I told her that I had worked for the church previously. She began to tell me in a very casual and polite way that she didn't think that the church was relevant anymore and that people were finding community in places like her café where friendships, connections and community were made. She told me quite confidently that we needed more cafes not churches. Another time I was at our neighborhood markets chatting with locals about their thoughts around happiness. This was for a course I was running about the topic at our neighborhood center. The course did not talk about Christianity but looked at a very broad spirituality and also well-being practices. The course was a safe place for anyone to come and share their thoughts, however varied, about the deeper things in life. One person came up to me and was highly suspicious about what I was doing. "Are you from a religious organization?" he asked. "Where do you get your funding?" he shot at me. "How much does it cost?" he suspiciously asked. In the end, we had a good conversation about what I was doing and the meaning of happiness as he realized that I wasn't "selling" anything. However, I mention these two stories of locals in my community as examples of the context in which we now find ourselves in the West. People are suspicious, dismissive of the institutional church and struggle to see its relevance to their daily lives. Christians have tended to move to the suburbs and given up on the busy, noisy, often perceived "godless" city, need to see the city as a sacred space that needs more of our compassion, energy and presence.

The "Patient Ferment" of the Church

N.T Wright summarizes the mission of the church succinctly and beautifully by saying

> The mission of the church is nothing more nor less than the outworking, in the power of the Spirit, of Jesus' bodily resurrection, and thus the anticipation of the time when God will fill the earth with his glory, transform the old heavens and earth into the new, and raise his children from the dead to populate and rule over the redeemed world he has made.[2]

However, as I have argued, the Church has attempted to carry out this mission through an other-worldly spirituality. The church has displayed a sacred-secular divide and often a withdrawing from the world posture. This is contrary to a missional and urban spirituality. God is at work through his people in the neighborhood now, so place, time and space matter. Wright continues by saying

> Thus the church that takes sacred space seriously, not a retreat from the world bit as a bridgehead into it, will go straight from worshipping in the sanctuary into the council chamber- to debate matters of town planning, of harmonizing and humanizing beauty in architecture, in green spaces, in road traffic schemes, and...in environmental work, creative and healthy farming methods, and proper use of resources. If it is true, as I have argued, that the whole world is now God's holy land, we must not rest as long as that land is spoiled and defaced. This is not an "extra" to the church's mission. It is central.[3]

The mission of the church, gathered and scattered, is to embody the gospel locally, telling the story of the kingdom of God, challenging false narratives and offering the hope of eternal life to everyone. This must happen in a "this-worldly" fashion as Wright articulates so clearly.

---

[2] Wright, *Surprised by Hope*, 277.
[3] Ibid., 278.

An urban spirituality is this: worldly and missional. At the beginning of this book I mentioned that there are four characteristics of an urban spirituality; embodies the *missio Dei*, speaks to the peculiarities of the city, crafts practices to embody our faith and seeks the well-being of the city. As I have described in this book I have been attempting to live this out in my inner city context for a few years now. I have been trying to embody the mission of God in my urban neighborhood through practices that shape my faith as well as serve the community where I live. One thing that has been clear to me during this time is that living out this mission in the city happens very differently to the way many practitioners, church planters and ministers often describe. I often hear about church planting or engaging with the city in terms that sound more like a military campaign, a marketing strategy, or project management with targets, outcomes and goals to be accomplished. Speed, efficiency, pragmatism and a taste for the spectacular seem to be the values that are cherished. However, as I have been living in the inner city trying to work with what God is doing, I have found it to be a very slow, messy and profound work in which I have been caught up in the lives of people and the sometimes disorienting goings on of the community. It has so far been a work of love, *kenosis,* compassion, patience, faithfulness and discernment. Moreover, the work has sometimes been frustrating and mundane.

In *The Patient Ferment of the Early Church* Alan Kreider suggests that the early church understood the patience of God and this was reflected in the way that they were the church. He says, "The Christians believed that God is patient and that Jesus visibly embodied patience. And they concluded that they, trusting in God, should be patient-not controlling events, not anxious or in a hurry, and never using force to achieve their ends."[4] Moreover, he says that Christian witness was connected to this patience in the form of embodied behavior rather than verbal proclamations, evangelism strategies and church growth methodologies.

> The sources rarely indicate that the early Christians grew in number because they won arguments; instead they grew because their habitual behavior (rooted in patience) was distinctive and intriguing...They believed their habitus, their embodied behavior, was eloquent. Their behavior said what they believed; it was an enactment of their message. And the sources indicate that it was their habitus more than their ideas that appealed to the majority of the non-Christians who came to join them.[5]

This is closer to what I have been experiencing as an urban missionary in my neighborhood than many of the church planting, evangelism and church growth books that get a lot of attention today. Even books which espouse the missional paradigm, can display evidence of a more pragmatic and self-driven culture. However, this is not the way I have experienced God at work. This is not to say that God cannot or does not move quickly and accomplish tasks. But mostly, I see God at work in ways that are slow. The practices that I have spoken about are "slow practices" in the sense that they may not produce quick results but instead faithfulness is required. His ways also contain plenty of surprises and joy. As I have watched God at work, it has affected and shaped the way that I work.

---

[4] Alan Kreider, *The Patient Ferment of the Early Church*, (Grand Rapids: Baker Academic, 2016). Kindle Edition. Loc 243.
[5] Ibid.

Faithfulness, presence and discernment

Is faithfulness enough? I ask this question myself frequently. In a culture that is focused on speed, the spectacular and success, is faithfulness enough? Of course, the answer is yes, but living in a way that is consistent with faithfulness in community is more difficult. Often, I am tempted to move more quickly than God so that I can meet the demands of my culture, but each time something pulls me back towards faithfulness and trust in God's presence, call and work.

Ministry in the urban neighborhood needs to engage in a better theology and practice of faithfulness. James Davison Hunter in his book *To Change the World*, grounds a theology of faithful presence in the incarnation. He says,

> For the Christian, if there is human flourishing, in a world such as ours, it begins with God's word of love becoming flesh in us, is embodied in us, enacted through us and a trust is forged between the word spoken and the reality to which it speaks, to the realities to which we speak and the realities to which we the church point. In all, presence and place matter decisively.[6]

In the same way that God loved us by putting on flesh and "showing up" in the world, we also need to embody the gospel in our neighborhoods. This incarnational spirituality resonates in the urban space where being grounded, connected and engaged is so important as I have said in this book. Hunter highlights for us that the incarnation is no mere interesting theological concept but is instead evidence of God's love and intimacy shown towards us. God's love is "Commitment that is active not passive, intentional not accidental,

---

[6] James Davison Hunter, *To Change the World: The Irony, Tragedy and Possibility of Christianity in the Late Modern World* (Oxford: Oxford University Press, 2010), 241.

covenantal not contractual." God is with us wholeheartedly.[7] So then, if God has shown his "wholehearted" commitment to us in such an all-encompassing way, we must imitate this in our urban neighborhoods. Urban neighborhoods are beautiful and broken places that need us to display this kind of intimacy, wholeheartedness and faithfulness. Our neighborhoods are perfect places to live out this kind of faithfulness because of proximity and presence. We are present to our context and we dwell there, so we have a relationship with it in a way that a visitor does not. It is easy to be faithful to a cause in theory, but to embody wholehearted love towards the people who we interact with every day is a real measure of our faith. Again, the challenge for us is to live out what we preach from our platforms.

Living out this faithfulness and "wholehearted" love means being present and always being sensitive to what God is doing in the community where we live. This requires discerning the movement of the Spirit in our neighborhood. Once we believe that God does not forsake the city but instead that it is as much a sacred space as any mountaintop, river or hillside, we can begin to trust that God has gone before us and is very interested in welcoming us into joining with his work there. Alan Roxburgh agrees that the church has been too ecclesiocentric and must commit itself to the work of discerning God in the community in which it is placed. He suggests five practices that the church can engage in which are less ecclesially based and more broadly applied. The five practices are "Listening: attending to God, one another, and our neighborhoods. Discerning: Discovering where the Spirit is inviting us to join

---

[7] Ibid., 243.

with God in our neighborhoods. Testing: engaging in simple actions to join with God in the neighborhood. Reflection: Gathering to ask, What did we do? What are we learning? Where did we see God at work? Deciding: Determining what are the new ways we will not join with God in the neighborhood."[8]

As we begin to understand that the church is one aspect of the ecosystem of the neighborhood, and as we shift from asking "What is God doing in the church?" to "What is God doing in the neighborhood?" we begin to see God's extensive vision for our society unfold before our eyes. We even begin to realise that God's vision is rather more expansive than we once thought. All of a sudden, the church becomes one aspect of the kingdom rather than the only place where we see God at work. The gospel then becomes more about the restoration of our universe rather than simply the church as an end. We begin to understand that the church's task is to carry out God's mission rather than being the mission itself.

As we live out some of the urban spirituality practices mentioned in this book my hope is that an indigenous church or faith(ful) communities will emerge as we faithfully put these disciplines into practice. As we embody discernment, kenosis, incarnation, and a Trinitarian spirituality God will shape us into disciples that are suited to an urban environment and who will be a revelation of his work. We become witnesses to the kingdom of God come to our earth and present in our very neighborhoods. As I have argued in this book, this is not

---

[8] Alan Roxburgh, *Joining God, Remaking Church, and Changing the World: The New Shape of the Church in Our Time*, (New York: Morehouse Publising 2015). Kindle Edition. Loc 1206.

only about our formation but also about us shaping the environment in which we live. Living holy in the city is not about removal from the mess of life but instead about imitating our God who is "the Holy one in our midst" (Isaiah 12:6). We enter into the mess in order to make something beautiful from it. As we embody the gospel, discern the Spirit and more people encounter the good news of Jesus, my hope is that the church will emerge from the ecological web of the neighborhood. Ultimately, the church will contribute to this community network representing the broader work of Gods reign.

This kind of living out of our faith or spirituality is what Michael Gorman has called an "abide and go"[9] spirituality and what I have been outlining in this book. It is a faith that is not removed from this world but instead engages with our world. It does not separate the sacred and secular but rather sees that all things even the city, are consecrated by God. And primarily, an abide and go spirituality is about showing the hospitality of God in the day-to-day events and people that we encounter in our busy lives. Instead of retreating and "spending time with God" before we go out into our world to welcome and serve, we believe that service is spiritual and as we serve we encounter God. God is already active in our world and wants to meet us there in the streets, parks and places of our neighborhoods. In this way, our faith is shaped. In this way, we are witnesses to God's kingdom come on earth.

---

[9] Michael Gorman, "Abide and Go: John's Missional Spirituality " In *School of Theology Payton Lectures: Gospel of John And the Mission of God* (Fuller Seminary: 2016).

How do we live this kind of holy life in the city? How do we embody the relevant aspects of ancient monastic communities and apply them to the urban context? Do such things as *urban monks* exist? Often, I see that our world is better at embodying this kind of engagement with communities in the city than Christians are. One member of our inner-city community passed away some time ago and he was remembered for his activism, care and persistence in bringing justice to the urban neighborhood. He was a contentious figure, a "character", and I don't know where he stood regarding his faith but a newspaper article at the time of his death honoured him and quoted his rationale for his activity in the urban context where he lived for many years.

> What do I get out of it? It's a community; it's a family; you're part of a structure. Call it what you like you're part of the area that you live in. When people ask why I become involved in community work like this, I tell them that it's because I'd like to think that one day someone would help me...if you have any concern for the people around you, if you'd like to have friends, be able to nod to people as you go down the street and say hello to them...it's only a small extension from that to ask them how they're feeling today and having a brief conversation with them. It's about being friendly; talking to people. In the inner city in particular, it can be a very lonely place if you don't want to talk to people. So don't be scared-it can't bite you![10]

I see compassion, intentionality and a deep understanding of the issues and ecology of the neighborhood in these words from a loved member in my community. I don't, however, often see this kind of intentionality, understanding or faithfulness among church communities in the city. It seems that increasingly we are more interested in our internal church machinery or even running away from the city. We concern ourselves with the details of pastoral care of church members, keeping over-fed Christians comfortable and

---

[10] "Community Gathers to Remember Ross Leslie Smith (1941-2016)," *South Sydney Herald*, December 2016, 7.

preaching a gospel that is often disembodied from the context in which we are meant to be embodying it. Therefore, we live out a faith or spirituality that is other-worldly and dualistic.

Despite this sad observation, there is hope. I have great hope for the church today, as do many others. The hope is not in our own efforts but in a God who is faithful, wholeheartedly devoted to us, and whose mercies are fresh for us every day even though we frequently stumble and fall. God is unstoppable. God will build his kingdom. A prayer I have been praying recently is for the atmosphere of heaven to increasingly infiltrate my neighborhood. Join me in praying this for your neighborhood and may Father, Son and Spirit bless you as you move with them in bringing love, truth, hope and beauty to your community.

Allow more and more thoughts
of Your thinking to come into our hearts,
Day by day,
till there shall at last be an open road
between you and us,
and Your angels may go up and down among us,
so that we may be in your heaven,
even while we are upon Your earth. Amen.
(Liminal Space, Where Earth and Heaven Meet).[11]

---

[11] The Northumbria Community, *Celtic Daily Prayer Book One; the Journey Begins* (London: William Collins, 2015), 185.

References

Augsburger, David. *Dissident Discipleship*. Grand Rapids: Brazos Press, 2006.

Aw, Tash. "Sail." *A Public Space*, no. 13 Summer (2011): 122-143.

Bevans, Stephen. "God inside Out: Towards a Missionary Theology of the Holy Spirit." *International Bulletin of Missionary Research* 22, no. 3 (1998): 102-5.

Bolsinger, Tod. *It Takes a Church to Raise a Christian: How the Community of God Transforms Lives*. Grand Rapids MI: Brazos Press, 2004.

Bosch, David. *A Spirituality of the Road*. Scottdale PA: Herald Press, 1979.

Bosch, David. *Transforming Mission: Paradigm Shifts in Theology of Mission*. Maryknoll: Orbis Books, 1991.

Bouma-Prediger, S., and Brian Walsh. *Beyond Homelessness: Christian Faith in a Culture of Displacement*. Grand Rapids: Eerdmans, 2008.

Capaque, George. "Spirituality for Asian Contexts: The Philippines and Beyond." In *Walking with God: Christianity in the Asian Context*, edited by Karen Hollenbeck-Wuest Charles Ringma. Manila: OMF, 2014.

Carson, Don. *The Gospel According to John*. Grand Rapids: Eerdmans, 1991.

Celtic Daily Prayer: From the Northumbria Community. New York: HarperOne, 2002.

Christopher Smith, John Pattison. *Slow Church: Cultivating Community in the Patient Way of Jesus*. Downers Grove: Intervarsity Press, 2014. Kindle Edition.

Clarke, Ron. *Jesus Unleashed*. Eugene: Cascade, 2013. Kindle Edition.

Community, The Northumbria. *Celtic Daily Prayer Book One; the Journey Begins*. London: William Collins, 2015.

"Community Gathers to Remember Ross Leslie Smith (1941-2016)." *South Sydney Herald*, December 2016, 7.

Connor, Benjamin. *Practicing Witness: A Missional Vision of Christian Practices*. Grand Rapids: Eerdmans, 2011. Kindle Edition.

Craig Van Gelder, and Dwight J. Zscheile. *The Missional Church in Perpective: Mapping Trends and Shaping the Conversation*. Grand Rapids: Baker Academic, 2011. Kindle Edition.

Cunningham, David. *These Three Are One: The Practice of Trinitarian Theology*. Oxford: Blackwell, 1998.

Davey, Andrew. *Urban Christianity and Global Order: Theological Resources for an Urban Future*. London: SPCK, 2001.

Dykstra, Craig and Dorothy Bass. "A Way of Thinking About a Way of Life." In *A Way of Thinking about a Way of Life*, edited by Dorothy Bass. San Fancisco: Jossey-Bass, 2010.

Foster, Tim. *The Suburban Captivity of the Church: Contextualising the Gospel for Post-Christian Australia* Moreland VIC: Acorn Press, 2014. Kindle Edition.

Franke, John. "God Is Love." In *Trinitarian Theology for the Church*, edited by David Lauber Daniel treier. Downers Grove, IL: Intervarsity Press, 2009.

Friesen, Dwight. "Formation in the Post-Christendom Era: Exilic Practices and Missional Identity." In *The Gospel after Christendom: New Voices, New Cultures, New Expressions*, edited by Ryan Bolger. Grand Rapids: Baker Publishing, 2012.

Galilea, Segundo. *The Way of Living Faith: A Spirituality of Liberation*. New York: Harper and Row, 1988.

Gittins, Anthony. *Bread for the Journey: The Mission of Transformation and Transformation of Mission*. Maryknoll: Orbis Books, 1993.

Goheen, Michael. *A Light to the Nations: The Missional Church and the Biblical Story*. Grand Rapids: Baker Academic, 2011.

Gooder, Paula. *Body: Biblical Spirituality for the Whole Person*. London: SPCK, 2016.

Gorman, Michael. *Cruciformity: Paul's Narrative Spirituality of the Cross*. Grand Rapids: Eerdmans, 2001.

Gorman, Michael. "The This-Worldliness of the New Testament's Otherworldly Spirituality." In *The Bible and Spirituality* edited by J. McConville A. Lincoln, L. Pietersen Eugene OR: Cascade, 2013.

Gorman, Michael. "Abide and Go: John's Missional Spirituality " In *School of Theology Payton Lectures: Gospel of John And the Mission of God*. Fuller Seminary, 2016.

Gornick, Vivian. *The Odd Woman and the City*. Carlton: Nero, 2015. Kindle Edition.

Gorringe, Tim. *A Theology of the Built Environment: Justice,Empowerment,Redemption*. Cambridge: Cambridge University Press, 2002.

Greenman, Jeffrey. "Spiritual Formation in Theological Perspective." In *Life in the Spirit: Spiritual Formation in Theological Perspective*, edited by Jeffrey Greenman. Downers Grove, IL: IVP Academic, 2010.

Guder, Darrell. *Incarnation and the Church's Witness*. Harrisburg: Trinity Press International, 1999.

Guder, Darrell. "Worthy Living: Work and Witness from the Perspective of Missional Church Theology." *Word and World* 25, no. 4 (Fall 2005): 424-432.

Gunton, Colin. *The Promise of Trinitarian Theology*. Edinburgh: T&T Clark, 1991.

Hastings, Ross. *Missional God, Missional Church*. Downer's Grove: Intervarsity Press, 2012. Kindle Edition.

Hauerwas, Stanley. *Vision and Virtue*. Notre Dame IN: Fides Publications, 1974.

Hauerwas, Stanley. *Brazos Theological Commentray on the Bible: Matthew*. Grand Rapids: Brazos, 2006.

Heath, Elaine. *Missional, Monastic, Mainline: A Guide to Starting Missional Micro-Communities in Historiclaly Mainline Traditions*. Eugene: Cascade, 2014.

Helland, R. and L. Hjalmarson. *Missional Spirituality: Embodying God's Love from the inside Out*. Downer's Grove: IVP, 2011. Kindle Edition.

Hill, Graham. *Global Church: Reshaping Our Conversations, Renewing Our Mission, Revitalizing Our Churches*. Downers Grove: IVP Academic, 2016.

Hirsch, Alan, and Deb Hirsch. *Untamed: Reactivating a Missional Form of Discipleship*. Gand Rapids: Baker Books, 2010.

Holt, Simon Carey. *God Next Door: Spirituality and Mission in the Neighbourhood*. Brunswick East: Acorn Press, 2007. Kindle Edition.

Hunsberger, George. *The Church between Gospel and Culture*, Edited by Craig Van Gelder and George Hunsberger. Grand Rapids MI: Baker Books, 1996.

Hunter, George. *The Celtic Way of Evangelism: How Christianity Can Reach the West Again*. 2 ed., 2010. Kindle Edition.

Hunter, James Davison. *To Change the World: The Irony, Tragedy and Possibility of Christianity in the Late Modern World*. Oxford: Oxford University Press, 2010.

Inge, John. *A Christian Theology of Place*. Hampshire: Ashgate, 2003.

Jacobs, Jane. *The Death and Life of American Cities*. New York: Vintage reissue edition, 1992.

Jacobsen, Eric. *Sidewalks in the Kingdom: New Urbanism and the Christian Faith*. Grand Rapids:MI: Brazos Press, 2003. Kindle Edition.

Jay Pathak, Dave Runyon. *The Art of Neighboring: Building Genuine Relationships Right Outside Your Door*. Grand Rapids: Baker Publishing, 2012. Kindle Edition.

Jenson, Matt. *The Gravity of Sin: Augustine, Luther and Barth on 'Homo Incurvatus in Se'*. London: T&T Clark, 2007.

Jones, Barry. *Dwell: Life with God for the World*. Downers Grove Il: Intervarsity Press, 2014.

Kardong, Terrance. *The Bendictines*. Wilmington: M. Glazier, 1988.

Kemmis, Daniel. *Community and the Politics of Place*. Norman Oklahoma: University of Oklahoma Press, 1990.

Kenneson, Phillip. *Life on the Vine: Cultivating the Fruit of the Spirit in Chrisitan Community*. Downer's Grove: Intervarsity Press, 1999.

Kreider, Alan. *The Patient Ferment of the Early Church*. Grand Rapids: Baker Academic, 2016. Kindle Edition.

L'Engle, Madeleine. *Walking on Water: Reflections of Faith and Art*. Colorado Springs: WaterBrook, 2001.

Laing, Olivia. *The Lonely City: Adventures in the Art of Being Alone*. NYC: Picador, 2016.

Langdon, Phillip. *A Better Place to Live*. Amherst: University of Massachusetts Press, 1994.

Lewis, C.S. *Miracles*. New York: Macmillan, 1947.

Mackay, Hugh. *What Makes Us Tick? The Ten Desires That Drive Us*. Sydney: Hachette, 2010.

Mackay, Hugh. *The Good Life*. Sydney: Macmillan, 2013.

McAlpine, William. *Sacred Space for the Missional Church: Engaging Culture through the Built Environment*. Eugene: Wipf and Stock, 2011.

McKnight, Scot. *The King Jesus Gospel: The Original Good News Revisited*. Grand Rapids: Zondervan, 2011. Kindle Edition.

Missional Church:A Vision for the Sending of the Church in North America, edited by Darrell Guder. Grand Rapids MI: Eerdmans, 1998. Kindle Edition.

Newman, Elizabeth. *Untamed Hospitality*. Grand Rapids MI: Brazos Press, 2007.

Norris, Kathleen. *The Quotidian Mysteries: Laundry, Liturgy and "Women's Work*. Mahwah: Paulist Press, 1998.

Pascal Bazzell, and Amelia Ada-Bucog. "Subversive Urban Spirituality in Asian Cities: Reimagining Spiritual and Missional Practices in Filipino Urban Poor Centres." In *Walking with God: Chrisitan Spirituality in the Asian Context*. , edited by Karen Hollenbeck-Wuest Charles Ringma. Manlia: OMF, 2014.

Pietersen, Lloyd. *Reading the Bible after Christendom*. Milton Keynes: Paternoster, 2011. Kindle Edition.

Pohl, Christine. *Making Room: Recovering Hospitality as a Christian Tradition*. Eerdmans: Grand Rapids MI, 1999.

Robinson, Marilynne. *The Givenness of Things*. London: Virago, 2015.

Roxburgh, Alan. "Practices of Christian Life- Forming and Performing a Culture." *Journal of Missional Practice* Autumn, (2012).

Roxburgh, Alan. *Joining God, Remaking Church, and Changing the World: The New Shape of the Church in Our Time.* New York: Morehouse Publising 2015. Kindle Edition.

Russell, Letty, J.Shannon Clarkson, and Kate M. Ott. *Just Hospitality: God's Welcome in a World of Difference.* Louisville: Westminster John Knox Press, 2009.

Scandrette, Mark. *Practicing the Way of Jesus: Life Together in the Kingdom of Love.* Downers Grove: IVP, 2011. Kindle Edition.

Sheldrake, Phillip. *The Spiritual City:Theology,Spirituality and the Urban.* Chichester,West Sussex: John Wiley and Sons, 2014. Kindle Edition.

Smith, Gordon. "Spirituality That Takes Creation Care Seriously " In *Walking with God: Christian Spirituality in the Asian Context*, edited by Karen Hollenbeck-Wuest Charles Ringma. Manila: OMF, 2014.

Smith, James K.A. *Desiring the Kingdom: Worship, Worldview and Cultural Formation.* Gran Rapids: Baker Academic, 2009.

Snyder, C. Arnold. *Following in the Footsteps of Christ: The Anabaptist Tradition.* London: Darton Longman and Todd, 2004.

Tan, Chade-Meng. *Joy on Demand: The Art of Discovering the Happiness Within.* New York: Harper Collins, 2016.

Taylor, Charles. *A Secular Age.* Cambridge MA: Harvard University Press, 2007.

The Rule of St Benedict in English, Edited by Timothy Fry. Collegeville: The Liturgical Press, 1982.

Volf, Miroslav. *A Public Faith: How Followers of Christ Should Serve the Common Good.* Grand Rapids: Brazos, 2011.

Wiesel, Elie. "Longing for Home." In *The Longing for Home*, edited by L S Rouner. Notre Dame Indiana: University of Notre Dame Press, 1996.

Wilkens, Steve and Mark L.Sanford. *Hidden Worldviews: Eight Cultural Stories That Shape Our Lives.* Downers Grove Il: IVP Academic, 2009.

Wilson, Gerald. "Songs for the City: Interpreting Biblical Psalms in an Urban Context." In *Psalms and Practice: Worship, Virtue and Authority.* Minnesota: Michael Glazier, 2001.

Wright, N.T. *Surprised by Hope: Rethinking Heaven, the Resurrection and the Mission of the Church.* NYC: Harper One, 2008.

Wright, Tom. *Virtue Reborn.* London: SPCK, 2010.

Author Bio

Rev. Dr. Karina Kreminski works at Morling College Sydney Australia as Lecturer in Missional Studies

Before this she was the Senior Pastor of Community Life Church Cherrybrook and was ordained in 2002. She ministered there for 13 years. Karina completed her doctorate in missional studies focusing on the formation of a missional church and missional spirituality. She has also been involved in denominational leadership serving on various boards.

Karina blogs regularly for Mission Alliance and in other forums. She also preaches at churches, conferences, and events and enjoys mentoring leaders.

Karina is a missionary and community worker in the inner city of Sydney and is in the early stages of starting a faith community there.

Printed in Great Britain
by Amazon